# YOUR EUCHARISTIC IDENTITY

FATHER GREGORY PINE, O.P.

# Your Eucharistic Identity

## A Sacramental Guide to the Fullness of Life

IGNATIUS PRESS SAN FRANCISCO

Cover design by Enrique J. Aguilar


ISBN 978-1-62164-796-6 (PB)
ISBN 978-1-64229-359-3 (eBook)
Library of Congress Control Number 2025934378
Printed in the United States of America ♾

# CONTENTS

## Chapter 1

# Receiving the Gift

In the course of our human story, we are all confronted by the question of identity. We want to make sense of ourselves and of our experience, and there wells up within each of us the conviction that there is sense to be made. Along the way, we have to work through our personal doubts and worries. And as we advance, we seek a sense of self, a sense of fit, a sense of purpose. Who are we? What are we for? Honestly, we need to know! If we could just figure it out, then we could live!

This question of identity has become more complicated in recent years as approaches to sexuality and gender have taken on new complexity. In the midst of our cultural moment, we might be tempted just to set our doubts and worries aside. After all, maybe all of this talk about identity is a mere fad or trend. Perhaps it is better not to engage. That may be so, but before we move on, what if we were to try to answer the question *well*? What if we were to dig into the Christian tradition and unearth hidden riches? This book is an attempt to do just that, and the proposal is simple:

> Our identity is disclosed and bestowed in a life of Eucharistic worship. If we want to know who we are and what we are for, there is both revelation and grace to be had from our Eucharistic belief and practice.

I encourage you to read this book with the conviction that Christ will answer the question of identity in accord with His wisdom and love, albeit in His own mysterious way. He may not always provide the *clear responses* we often prefer, but He will always give us *Himself*. And herein lies the core of our identity. Christ does not want to give us just *any* identity. He wants to give us His identity. Through a life of Eucharistic worship, we become like Christ, for in receiving Him, we receive His identity as our own.

From the sacrament of the altar, Christ prompts us to voice our doubts and worries. So, too, He promises to address them. Saint John Paul II writes in *Salvifici Doloris*, "For Christ does not answer directly and he does not answer in the abstract this human questioning about the meaning of suffering. Man hears Christ's saving answer as he himself gradually becomes a sharer in the sufferings of Christ."[1] What the Holy Father says about suffering in general applies to the suffering borne of our search for an identity. Christ intends to respond to our questions, and He does so by sharing Himself with us, by welcoming us into His life.

This book sets forward different features of Eucharistic belief and practice as a way to help us receive our Eucharistic identity. In this first chapter, we will focus on God's gift of life. Our identity is beautifully framed by the facts that we are from God and for God. In the second chapter, we see what it looks like to unpack this gift. Contemplating Christ's place in the most blessed Trinity, we will find there a life intended for us. In the third chapter, we will consider *how* God pours His infinite life into the finite vessel of our humanity. The key is contact, as God

[1]John Paul II, *Salvifici Doloris* (February 11, 1984), §26.

touches us—soul and body—through faith and the sacraments. In the fourth chapter, we will begin meditating on the Eucharist in earnest. Sacramentality serves as our starting point. In short, the Mass addresses us and draws us with signs.

The next three chapters ponder the principal signs of the Mass. Chapter 5 considers the sign of the twofold consecration. The separation of Christ's body and blood commemorates and applies His one, saving sacrifice. Furthermore, we will see how His sacrifice makes possible *our* sacrifice. Chapter 6 turns to the sign of the Eucharistic elements themselves, namely, bread and wine. The appearances of food and drink mediate a spiritual nourishment and delight born of the grace of charity—that sublime love which God intends for each of us. Chapter 7 looks even more closely at how the elements are made. The coming together of bread and wine causes the coming together of Christians in the body of Christ. In an eighth and final chapter, we will see how this sacramental vision can become part of "everyday life". Ultimately, these signs are meant to become *daily bread* for each of us.

## Receiving or Crafting

Throughout the book, I will emphasize the importance of *receiving* our identity. In fact, a posture of receptivity is at the foundation of our Eucharistic belief and practice. The Eucharist is God's *gift*. As we approach the altar to receive the Lord's body and blood, we endeavor to receive worthily and devoutly. As strange as it may seem, it is in receiving Him and possessing Him that we come to receive and to possess ourselves. In "getting" God, we "get" ourselves in turn. Clearly, we do not go to God *in order* to get ourselves. We go to God to get Him and are pleasantly surprised to find that we get ourselves as well. But, to further this transformation, I will return often to the idea of *receiving* our identity through a worthy and devout participation in the life of Eucharistic worship.

Now, that all sounds wonderful, but we recognize immediately how very difficult it can be to *receive* an identity. What if, for instance, we have not always received good things in life? What if we have experienced profound loss? What if we have been exposed to acute physical, emotional, or psychological trauma? How can we be expected to receive an identity when life can prove so terrible for so many people?

Many of us have to wrestle with these questions—if not for ourselves, then for a family member or a friend. Many people find it so hard to receive their identities from a God they do not know or do not trust. Either they do not think to ask; or they worry about losing control; or they feel vulnerable broaching the question. Whatever the reason, many people find it practically impossible to receive their identities from God before the prospect of frustration or manipulation. In the circumstances, it is no surprise that they choose to get on with their lives and *craft* identities of their own.

This turn from receiving an identity to crafting an identity has sent many men and women down paths of profound sadness, loneliness, and anxiety. In an atmosphere charged with ideology, it is exceedingly difficult to see the issues with any clarity. As individuals struggle with the effects of psycho-sexual trauma or personal disintegration, the culture promises deliverance from rejection and misunderstanding. And so, for many people, it seems like an eminently sensible option to go in for the latest recommendation. But when the dust settles, many find that their choices have only yielded further confusion and revulsion. Nothing has changed, and if it has, it has only gotten worse.

As we witness the terrible damage done to so many lives, the question of identity arises with even greater urgency. Really, who are we? Seriously, what are we for? Our very lives depend upon it! If we are going to get anywhere, we have to be honest from the outset. There is no sense in downplaying the difficulty. Asking these questions of identity is *hard*. If we are sincere in our struggle, the answers we hear back will probably challenge us. Part of the purpose of this book is to help us overcome our hesitancy and to ask for our God-given lives with renewed fervor. Receiving our true identity will probably be at least a little bit painful. It will mean dealing with our weaknesses and wounds. It will mean pushing our limits. At times, the effort will seem entirely beyond us, but we draw strength from the assurance that Christ will not cease giving us Himself. Day in and day out, He recalls us to His fidelity, His constancy, even as He renews His offering at the altar of sacrifice.

## The Prodigal Son

The difficulty that many experience in receiving their identity is not a recent phenomenon. It is a perennial feature of our fallen condition. For as long as we can remember, we have felt a draw toward crafting an identity for ourselves. In what follows, we will look at two foundational narratives from the Sacred Scriptures that shed light on our human condition and begin to light up a way forward.

As members of the human community, we are constantly confronting the temptation to turn to ourselves, to wander off, to craft our own identity. The Lord, in His great love for us, has foreseen this temptation. What is more, He saves us from it. The parable of the prodigal son gives us a beautiful insight into how. Let's read the parable in its entirety:

> And [Jesus] said, "There was a man who had two sons; and the younger of them said to his father, 'Father, give me the share of property that falls to me.' And he divided his living between them. Not many days later, the younger son gathered all he had and took his journey into a far country, and there he squandered his property in loose living. And when he had spent everything, a great famine arose in that country, and he began to be in want. So he went and joined himself to one of the citizens of that country, who sent him into his fields to feed swine. And he would gladly have fed on the pods that the swine ate; and no one gave him anything. But when he came to himself he said, 'How many of my father's hired servants have bread enough and to spare, but I perish here with hunger! I will arise and go to my father, and I will say to him, "Father, I have sinned against heaven and before you; I am no longer worthy to be called your son; treat me as one of your hired servants."' And he arose and came to his father. But while he was yet at a distance, his father saw him and had compassion, and ran and embraced him and kissed him. And the son said to him, 'Father, I have sinned against heaven and before you; I am no longer worthy to be called your son.' But the father said to his servants, 'Bring quickly the best robe, and put it on him; and put a ring on his hand, and shoes on his feet; and bring the fatted calf and kill it, and let us eat and make merry; for this my son was dead, and is alive again; he was lost, and is found.' And they began to make merry.
>
> "Now his elder son was in the field; and as he came and drew near to the house, he heard music and dancing. And

> he called one of the servants and asked what this meant. And he said to him, 'Your brother has come, and your father has killed the fatted calf, because he has received him safe and sound.' But he was angry and refused to go in. His father came out and entreated him, but he answered his father, 'Behold, these many years I have served you, and I never disobeyed your command; yet you never gave me a kid, that I might make merry with my friends. But when this son of yours came, who has devoured your living with harlots, you killed for him the fatted calf!' And he said to him, 'Son, you are always with me, and all that is mine is yours. It was fitting to make merry and be glad, for this your brother was dead, and is alive; he was lost, and is found.'" (Lk 15:11–32)

This precious passage from the Gospel of Luke gives us a look into our spiritual predicament. Let's turn first to the younger son. Clearly, he has not found his fit. He is alienated from his father and from himself. To ask for his inheritance "is tantamount to wishing his father dead". In his own mind he thinks that, if he is really going to experience life, he needs to cut ties and leave. And so, he renounces his sonship and crafts for himself a new existence.

Having journeyed to a far country, he enjoys a fleeting bliss. His "loose living" does not even occupy a full verse. The evangelist passes over the lurid details almost entirely. Instead, we hear of a tragic fall and a terrible emptiness. He has lost hold of his human dignity and found himself among the swine. In trying to dictate the terms of his own life, he has lost everything. And yet, as another author observes, "[The] sense of lost dignity makes him ... aware that he is indeed the *son* who had dignity to lose."[2]

[2] Henri Nouwen, *The Return of the Prodigal Son* (New York: Doubleday, 1992), 49.

As he comes to his senses, it is as if he is trying to formulate a question: "How many of my father's hired servants have bread enough and to spare, but I perish here with hunger!" At this point, the question is still rhetorical. The younger son is curious about his experience, but he is not yet asking someone else (or Someone Else) for answers. Nevertheless, he recognizes the absurdity of his state and resolves to do something about it. And so, he turns his face homeward.

As the younger son rehearses his apology, it is evident that his conversion is incomplete. While he intends to acknowledge his foolishness, he also expects to tell his father what will happen next: He is to be treated like a hired servant. But his plan fails to account for the offer of mercy. He has forgotten, or perhaps never known, his father's love. He is about to be reminded.

As we have seen, the younger son does not ask to be reinstated in his sonship. To do so would mean opening himself up to the grandeur of his vocation, making himself vulnerable to a love beyond the bounds of his present understanding. Fortunately though, his father does not wait for him to ask. The father reaffirms his love while cutting short his son's recital of what will happen next. The prodigal is clothed in the dignity of the household, the dignity of his sonship. His identity is clarified, conferred anew, by the one who gave him life.

How does the younger son respond? The passage does not say, but we can imagine. Perhaps he found it difficult to assume his robe, his ring, and his sandals and to partake of the fatted calf without embarrassment. Maybe he wanted to avoid notice or to re-integrate discreetly. He had already ruined his life once. Who is to say he would not do it again? All the hubbub might have made him nervous at the prospect of further failure. At this stage, his identity is fragile—better not to make much of it.

The indignation of the elder son at his brother's return illustrates an alternative (but equally mistaken) response to the father's love. For, while he chooses to stay at home, he still lives far from the father. Though he abides by the father's rules, he does not know the father's love. And, thus, he does not know himself. In fact, he has no idea who he is. His identity is fragile. His exasperation is a symptom of his alienation. Recall how the three parables told in Luke 15 (the lost sheep, the lost coin, and the prodigal son) are all told in response to Pharisaic murmuring: "This man receives sinners and eats with them" (Lk 15:2). The older son cannot conceive of the father's mercy because he remains far from the father's love.

All throughout their lives, both sons were surrounded by their father's affection. The younger son walks away from that affection, and the elder son simply refuses to see it. Clearly, it is hard work to receive our lives from God, to come into possession of our God-given identities. Regardless of whether we choose to wander away or to stay behind, all of us must work to embrace the Father's love. We must bring our question before the One who gives life to His sons and daughters with the trust that He intends to answer.

## The Garden

Truth be told, it might have been easier to receive our lives had things played out differently in the beginning. As we know, our alienation and need for salvation date back to an original rejection of God's gift. The suspicion that we each feel before the promise of life everlasting is a suspicion that first wormed its way into the hearts of Adam and Eve. For, though our first parents were created in perfect relation to

God, it fell to them to ratify their perfect relation. In short, they had to choose to receive their lives. Here, in the lives of Adam and Eve, the whole drama of our identity is already present. Before the younger son ever wandered off or the elder son ever seethed with resentment, our first parents experienced a most basic temptation. And it was their yielding that first threw our identity into confusion.

To get a better sense for our existential state, whether we are a younger son or an elder son, let's read the beginning of Genesis 3:

> Now the serpent was more subtle than any other wild creature that the LORD God had made. He said to the woman, "Did God say, 'You shall not eat of any tree of the garden'?" And the woman said to the serpent, "We may eat of the fruit of the trees of the garden; but God said, 'You shall not eat of the fruit of the tree which is in the midst of the garden, neither shall you touch it, lest you die.'" But the serpent said to the woman, "You will not die. For God knows that when you eat of it your eyes will be opened, and you will be like God, knowing good and evil." So when the woman saw that the tree was good for food, and that it was a delight to the eyes, and that the tree was to be desired to make one wise, she took of its fruit and ate; and she also gave some to her husband, and he ate. Then the eyes of both were opened, and they knew that they were naked; and they sewed fig leaves together and made themselves aprons.
>
> And they heard the sound of the LORD God walking in the garden in the cool of the day, and the man and his wife hid themselves from the presence of the LORD God among the trees of the garden. But the LORD God called to the man, and said to him, "Where are you?" And he said, "I heard the sound of you in the garden, and I was afraid, because I was naked; and I hid myself." He said, "Who told you that you were naked? Have you eaten of the tree

> of which I commanded you not to eat?" The man said, "The woman whom you gave to be with me, she gave me fruit of the tree, and I ate." Then the LORD God said to the woman, "What is this that you have done?" The woman said, "The serpent beguiled me, and I ate."

To appreciate what is going on here, we have to think back to the story of creation in the preceding two chapters. As God bestows life on our first parents, He also places conditions on their enjoyment thereof: "You may freely eat of every tree of the garden; but of the tree of the knowledge of good and evil you shall not eat, for in the day that you eat of it you shall die" (Gen 2:16–17). Christians throughout the centuries have read this passage as an invitation to *relationship*, specifically to a relationship of *dependence*. Man is created to live with God—to be from Him, through Him, and for Him. Our first parents were made to depend upon God, to look to Him for their understanding and enjoyment of the good life. Within the setting of these conditions, the scene is set for fulfillment, but on its periphery lies the possibility of disaster. And, as we know, disaster comes to pass.

Our first parents made it a mere five verses before transgressing the bounds set by God. And, wouldn't you know, their relationship with God was ruined by a doubt touching on identity. The confusion begins with a mistaken notion of *God's* identity. We see this especially in the conversation between Eve and the serpent. Notice how she exaggerates the divine command. Whereas God tells them not to *eat of* the tree, Eve says they cannot even *touch* it. Her severe interpretation of the law reveals a certain distrust of the lawgiver. Eve fails to make a clear connection between divine law and human happiness. In her mind, the prohibition is not so much the concrete expression of

God's solicitude as an arbitrary limitation to human expression. Whether it is eating or touching or something else, the law has constrained her freedom.

The serpent seizes this opportunity to drive a wedge between her and God: "You will not die. For God knows that when you eat of it your eyes will be opened, and you will be like God, knowing good and evil" (Gen 3:4–5). The serpent's words represent an offer of autonomy or self-sufficiency. If Adam and Eve could determine good and evil, that might mean moving *beyond* good and evil, beyond the need for God and His law. They could be a law unto themselves, like gods in the firmament. Thus, they could craft an identity for themselves, an identity of their own choosing.

We should not be shocked to learn that the serpent traffics in lies, but the precise nature of this lie is especially insidious. Effectively, the serpent convinced our first parents that they would inherit something that they *already had*. Because they enjoyed the life of grace, heaven was already spilling onto earth and into their souls. Even as they conversed with the serpent, they were receiving the divine life. Grace makes you like God, and so it follows that Adam and Eve were already like gods. Their identity is plain for us to see. They just had to ask for it and receive it from God, to be like gods in the way that *God* willed. Instead, their confusion about God's identity caused confusion about their own identity.

When they fell, our first parents began to suffer a new and terrible vulnerability. Their choice left them weak and wounded, exposed in a way they were never meant to be. They made loincloths out of fig leaves and turned from the God whom they no longer trusted. They lost their understanding of Him from whom, through whom, and for whom was their life, and in the process, they lost themselves as well.

The Fall reveals our own existential state with awful clarity. Like Adam and Eve, we have difficulty looking to the Father and trusting in His goodness. Struggling to receive our identity, we turn in on ourselves and craft an identity. In every generation, we are tempted to slouch toward the posture of our first parents as their sin becomes our own. We have all chosen not to receive our life from God as a gift; we have all chosen not to dwell in His abiding presence; we have all chosen not to look to Him for our identity. Instead, we have chosen to go it alone. In the garden, where the seed of all dysphoria was sown, we see the omen of our current confusion.

## Our Created (and Received) Identity

These stories show us that we cannot craft our own lives. Our identity will not sprout inorganically in alien soil. It must be rooted in its original source. That is to say, identity can only be had within a relationship, a relationship of dependence upon our loving God. God alone can say with certainty who we are and what we are for. He has created us on purpose, imparted to us a capacity for greatness, and destined us to share in His divine life. "He is not far from each one of us, for 'In him we live and move and have our being'.... 'For we are indeed his offspring'" (Acts 17:28). In God, we find our fit. By His grace, we can live as He lives; we can ask for and receive His identity as our own.

In testimony to the incredible gift of God's own life, Saint Paul writes, "For from him and through him and for him are all things" (Rom 11:36 [NABRE]). From, through, for.... We typically do not think much about little words, but these three are filled with meaning and bring answers to our questions. Where am I from? What am I for? What is life about? From, through, for ... Simple words speak sense into our state.

*From Him*

First, we are *from Him*, the Creator of heaven and earth, of all things visible and invisible. All things come from Him. We are not a mistaken by-product of cosmic processes. We are the result of God's choice, the fruit of His creative love. All things in their tremendous variety are from God, who provides for each thing in its individuality and uniqueness. The poet Gerard Manley Hopkins extols the Lord as the one who "fathers-forth" all things:

> All things counter, original, spare, strange;
> Whatever is fickle, freckled (who knows how?)
> With swift, slow; sweet, sour; adazzle, dim;
> He fathers-forth whose beauty is past change:
> Praise him.[3]

As the origin of our existence, God is the source of our identity and of the mission that flows from it. He lays the foundation of our lives by His concrete choice. Our unique identity is, first and foremost, a *gift*. It could have been otherwise or not at all. And yet, here we are. On this foundation, God entrusts us with all that we need in order to become the saints He intends. God knows how to give good gifts to His children, and He does! Our existence is testimony to the fact.

Truth be told, we cannot account for creation other than *as a gift*. Before time began, God lacked nothing in the

[3] Gerard Manley Hopkins, "Pied Beauty", in *Poems of Gerard Manley Hopkins*, ed. Robert Bridges (Oxford: Oxford University Press, 1948), 74.

fullness of His divine beatitude. His choice to create corresponds, not to any need or longing on His part, but to His generosity. He created us because He *thought we might like it.* He has a secret too good to keep, the secret of His divine life, and He divulges that secret in each of us. This is the fundamental mystery whispered on high in our heavenly homeland: God loves us into being. Our identity is His gift.

### *Through Him*

Not only from Him, we are also *through Him*. Creation describes a relationship of total dependence on God, whose love is ongoing in our lives. He does not just create us and then leave us to ourselves. He does not wind up the universe and then let it run. Rather, God remains intimately involved; He upholds "the universe by his word of power" (Heb 1:3). We are, right now, *being created*, and God is present to us. As a wise Dominican once wrote, "The very fact that a thing *is* means that God himself *is there* at the roots of its being."

Cradle a glass of water in your hand, and you will see what I mean. As much as that glass of water depends on your palm in order not to fall to the ground and shatter, so we rely, at every single moment, on God's ongoing choice for us. It requires involvement. It requires contact. One author contrasts God's craftsmanship to that of a carpenter. A carpenter fashions a chair out of wood. If he leaves his shop, the chair continues to exist. Why? Because it has the wood to "fall back on". Now, God fashions creatures out of nothing. If God were to "leave His shop", to stop working on His creature, it would have *nothing* to fall back on. It would cease to exist.

But God never "leaves His shop". As Christ reveals, "My Father is working still, and I am working" (Jn 5:17).

We are, always and everywhere, *through* Him. God is intimately present to each of us. He gives us existence. He gives us life. He gives us an openness to receive His divine life. And, in the offer of grace, God draws nearer still. God dwells in the saints as in a temple. By making progress in the life of grace, we receive His gift in all its fullness; we beautify the temple of our interior lives as we abide more fully in God's holy presence.

### *For Him*

Finally, we are *for Him*. As T. S. Eliot wrote, "In my beginning is my end."[4] As we have seen, God has not created us for just any old reason. He has created us to share in His divine life. He has created us for union with Him. God Himself is the goal, the end, the purpose of our life.

This begins to explain why our experience can be so disappointing or unsatisfying at times. We are made for the household of God. We are made for a bountiful banquet laid at the heavenly table. At present, we are hungry and thirsty for meaning. "Sir, give me this water, that I may not thirst, nor come here to draw" (Jn 4:15). We cannot help feeling unhappy with the world's meager fare, when our nature is made for more substantial food and drink, the food and drink of God. While here on earth, we only get intimations of the perfect fulfillment that lies in store.

The strength of our hunger and thirst testifies eloquently to the fact that we are made for God. Everything in the world that we see, hear, smell, taste, and touch, that we grasp at, cling to, reach for, think about— ... everything that is *not* God—will leave us wanting, "dumbstruck

[4] T. S. Eliot, *The Four Quartets* (Orlando: Harcourt, 1943), 23.

also with an ache nothing can satisfy".[5] Although it can be painful to sense the real limitation of all that is not God, it is a mercy lest we settle for anything less than our Creator's bounty. As Saint Augustine wrote, "Our hearts are restless till they rest in Thee."[6]

Our desire for God may be dulled or dampened by vice and sin, by distraction and dispersion, but it can never be wholly extinguished. So long as we live and breathe, we will always know that there is more to be had than we experience at present. Even our endless questioning and wandering is itself God's gift, a gift meant to orient us to His identity and ours.

## From, Through, and For Eucharistic Worship

From Him, through Him, and for Him. *This* is who we are. *This* is what we are for. We are from God, through God, and for God. What will we choose to do with this endowment? Evidently, we could reject it. We could wander off to a distant land, try to be gods, and craft our own identities. Many people do, but there is no fit to be found there, only endless drifting.

Alternatively, we could embrace it. Rather than setting off on our own or seeking an affected autonomy, we can consent to be from, through, and for Him with *abandon*. In Christ, God offers us an opportunity to return to our true identity, and He gives us the means to make the effort. In the fullness of time, He sent us His Son, who established the Church and instituted the seven sacraments. Here we

[5] Richard Wilbur, *New and Collected Poems* (Orlando: Harcourt, 1988), 41.

[6] Augustine of Hippo, *Confessions*, trans. F.J. Sheed (Indianapolis: Hackett, 2006), bk. 1.1.

discover the most precious resources for the journey before us. In these pages, we will focus on the greatest of these gifts—the Holy Eucharist. In this, "the source and summit of the Christian life", we have the indispensable means to live from, through, and for God.[7]

In the Eucharist, we live *from* God. At each Mass, we gather at the foot of the Cross. We gaze on Christ's broken body as blood and water flow from His wounded side. This saving tide gives birth to the Church. By His love poured out, Christ generates us anew as sons and daughters of God. In Eucharistic worship, we receive the gift of our supernatural life; we become more fully "from" God.

Again, in the Eucharist, we live *through* God. At holy Mass, we give thanks to God from whom comes "every good endowment and every perfect gift" (Jas 1:17). Our daily reliance upon His flesh strengthens us even as it makes us depend more wholly on Him. Just as in the natural order we perish without nourishment, so in the supernatural order we perish without the body and blood of our Lord Jesus Christ. In Holy Communion, we have solid food and refreshing drink for our pilgrimage.

Finally, in the Eucharist, we live *for* God. While Holy Communion is more nourishing and delightful than any other fare, it leaves us wanting more. God desires to welcome us gradually into His fullness. He has chosen to do so by a strict diet. The Eucharist gives us a foretaste of the heavenly feast even as it increases our appetite for beatitude. It is not enough to visit with God. We want to dwell with Him forever.

God has made us to participate in His very life. Indeed, we are from Him, through Him, and for Him; our holiness

[7] *Catechism of the Catholic Church*, 2nd ed. (Vatican City: Libreria Editrice Vaticana, 1997), §1324 (hereafter cited as *CCC*).

goes by way of these facts. If we hold on to each of these little words and the mysteries that they signify, we have a way to arrive at our Eucharistic identity. In the pages that follow, we behold how the Lord offers the perfect sustenance for our existential search. In the sacrament of the altar, we discover our particular place at the table. For though senses may be deceived, yet Truth speaking clearly by heavenly signs has a Word to say about who we are and what we are for.

# Chapter 2

# Living His Life

Our satisfaction with life depends on what expectations we bring to it, and there are plenty of opinions about what we should expect. Some say we should set high expectations: Shoot for the moon! Others say we should set low expectations: Everything in moderation! Still others say we should have no expectations: Live in the moment! Certainly, there are merits in each approach. But what kind of expectations should we have as Christians? What should we expect from a life of Eucharistic worship?

Admittedly, it is hard to say. Our lives are unpredictable, and the end is largely hidden from us. How can I anticipate tomorrow, much less my far-flung future? As the Letter of James reminds us, "[Y]ou do not know about tomorrow. What is your life? For you are a mist that appears for a little time and then vanishes" (Jas 4:13–14). Nevertheless, we can spell out *some* expectations. Even if our predictions are rather vague, God's promises are plenty clear.

## To Be Another Christ

In the Sacred Scriptures, God promises the Israelites all manner of good things: land, triumph over enemies, consolation, descendants, blessing, and much more besides.

There is a beautiful pedagogy to the way He reveals Himself. As He draws His people into relationship with Him, the fulfillment of His promises serves as concrete proof of His goodness. The people come to believe that their God can be trusted, that He provides for His beloved.

In our Lord Jesus Christ, this pedagogy is brought to perfection. Christ is the greatest promise that God ever kept. And so, as part of the fulfillment that Christ brings, we might expect Him to add assurances to those of the Old Testament. Instead, He seems to subtract assurances. We hear less of the land or this-worldly victory. Rather than a series of things, Christ promises—indeed, gives—just one thing: Himself. Christ promises to abide with us, to draw us into His life. He makes Himself available to be possessed and espoused. As wild as it sounds, He promises to give us a share in His Godhead and to make us like Him.

The Christian tradition refers to this sharing in divine life as *divinization* or *deification*. Let's be clear: We are not polytheists! We remain human beings. But through grace, we come to share in the intimate communion of Father, Son, and Holy Spirit. As the Apostle Peter writes, "His divine power has granted to us ... [to] become partakers of the divine nature" (2 Pet 1:3–4). What is more, this participation is specifically "Christ-shaped". Like irons plunged into the fire of divine love and forged after the manner of the Son, each of us glows with the light and heat of the Triune life as we are shaped to the likeness of Christ. Each of us is called to be another Christ in the bosom of the Father.

With this promise in mind, we can set our expectations for a life of Eucharistic worship. Christ does not promise emotional stability or psychological balance. He does not promise physical beauty or social acceptance. He does not promise earthly success or optimal outcomes. He promises us Himself. Other good things may follow in His train, but they will always be an afterthought. We should therefore approach Him and worship Him, not as a means of self-fulfillment, but in recognition that He is worthy. "But seek first his kingdom and his righteousness, and all these things shall be yours as well" (Mt 6:33).

To share in the life of Father, Son, and Holy Spirit, to be transformed into the image of God's only begotten Son, we will need God's help. No amount of human inquiry can imagine the possibility. No amount of effort can attain such heights. Mindful of our limitations, God comes to our assistance. Throughout salvation history, He gives us gifts to help us along the way. He gives us the law and the prophets. He gives us Christ and His Mother. He gives us the Church and the sacraments. Among these gifts, there is one gift that represents "the most precious possession which the Church can have in her journey through history".[1] This, of course, is the Eucharist. For "[in] the Eucharist, Christ is giving us *Himself* ... and God has nothing better to give than Himself."[2]

In the Blessed Sacrament, God gives us divine fare for the divine life, food and drink fit for heaven-dwellers. By the divinizing grace in His body and blood, Christ makes us like Himself and draws us into the communion of His Trinitarian life. By worshipping this mystery and receiving this sacrament, we take up our place—*His* place—and so assume our identity in God. "[God has] destined us in love to be his sons through Jesus Christ, according to the purpose of his will, to the praise of his glorious grace which he freely bestowed on us in the Beloved" (Eph 1:5–6). This is our Eucharistic expectation, set from all eternity.

[1] John Paul II, *Ecclesia de Eucharistia* (April 17, 2003), §9.

[2] Lawrence Feingold, *The Eucharist: Mystery of Presence, Sacrifice, and Communion* (Steubenville: Emmaus Academic, 2018), xxviii.

Divine life, really? It seems so grandiose. Is it possible to live this way? We can answer simply: yes.

Clearly, the divine life goes way beyond our humanity. Nevertheless, we are created for this life—for Trinitarian communion in union with our Lord Jesus Christ. We see this plan sketched out for us on the first page of Sacred Scripture: "Then God said, 'Let us make man in our image, after our likeness.' ... So God created man in his own image, in the image of God he created him; male and female he created them" (Gen 1:26–27). Image and likeness in what sense? Of course, this does not mean that you have God's nose or chin. We do not look like God. But already at our creation, we are somehow related to God. How so?

In short, we are created capable of communion with God. We have already seen that we are from, through, and for God. But we are also made open to, even *bent on*, real relationship with Him. To be in the image of God means, "I exist as a term of a relationship. I don't 'have' relationships; I am, relationally."[3] Apart from this capability, man ceases to be man.

In all of material creation, only we can boast of this bearing. A piece of quartz cannot assent to the faith. An oak tree cannot contemplate God's mercy. A squirrel cannot seek mystical union. *Man can.* We can cultivate a connection with God, precisely because God has made us like Himself and for Himself. He has fashioned us with an eye to communion.

But what kind of communion? In short, a communion of potentially infinite knowing and loving. Each of us is

[3] David Fagerberg, *Liturgical Mysticism* (Steubenville: Emmaus Academic, 2019), 45.

endowed with an intellect and a will, spiritual powers that set us apart from lower creatures and fit us for spiritual realities. These powers spur us on with an unbridled spiritual energy. It is not enough for us to know trivial facts about basketball or to love a favorite podcast with deep loyalty. We are broken open to the wholly true and the entirely good, to a vast world transcending our experience. We are made for the Infinite.

The image of God thus conducts us beyond our merely human horizon to divine heights. By God's grace working through our intellect and will, we can come to know and love God Himself. This is the relationship for which we were made. "Let me see your face, let me hear your voice, for your voice is sweet, and your face is comely" (Song 2:14). In His loving-kindness, God lets us know Him as He knows Himself and love Him as He loves Himself. This is the point of our existence. "Mystical union with God is the consummation of humankind."[4] We are patterned on the divine life and destined for entry into it. What then of this life?

## The Life of the Trinity

This is not an easy topic to tackle. (You will have noticed that many priests get a little nervous preaching on Trinity Sunday.) But the Blessed Trinity is our most basic doctrine, "the central mystery of Christian faith and life" (*CCC* 234)—so we have to meditate upon it if we want to know our identity as Christians. In this section, we will give a quick overview of Trinitarian theology, with the help of something familiar to us: the prayers of the Mass.

[4] Ibid., 32.

Every Sunday at Mass, Catholics stand and profess belief in: "one God, the Father Almighty", in "one Lord, Jesus Christ, the Only Begotten Son of God", and "in the Holy Spirit, the Lord, the Giver of life". There are four important truths to draw from this confession. First, we believe in one God. We are monotheists, not polytheists. Second, we believe that God is a Trinity of Persons—the Father is God, the Son is God, and the Holy Spirit is God. Third, we believe that these Persons are really distinct—the Father is not the Son, the Son is not the Holy Spirit, and the Holy Spirit is not the Father. Fourth, we believe that these Persons are "distinct from one another *in their relations of origin*" (*CCC* 254; italics added). These relations of origin get at what we mean by Trinitarian communion. From all eternity, the Father *begets* the Son, and the Father and Son *breathe forth* the Holy Spirit. These are the relationships on which we are patterned and for which we are destined. To help us enter deeper into this Trinitarian life, let's turn now to the teaching of Saint Augustine.

Saint Augustine was passionate about trying to understand the Blessed Trinity. He famously devised several analogies to describe the relations of origin among Father, Son, and Holy Spirit. Perhaps the most famous of these analogies is called the "analogy of Word and Love", in which Saint Augustine leverages examples taken from human thought and affection, those most potent activities unfolding within our minds and hearts. The analogy runs something like this: The Father knows Himself. Because He is a perfect knower, He knows Himself by one perfect thought or concept. We call this His Word. In His Word, God knows Himself exhaustively and comprehensively. Thus, the Word contains within itself the whole being of God. As you might imagine, it bursts with life, the very life of the Father. Indeed, the Word differs from the Father only in that it is "from" the Father. The Word is God from

God. "He reflects the glory of God and bears the very stamp of his nature" (Heb 1:3). The Word lacks nothing of the Father's infinite, eternal, and omnipotent life. As He comes from the Father (or is begotten by the Father), we call this Word the Son.

Gazing upon the Word begotten of His boundless life, the Father sees in Him a likeness and a loveliness. Here is one like Him. Here is one surpassing in goodness. So, too, gazing upon the Father from whom He comes forth, the Word—the Son—perceives a likeness and a loveliness. Here, again, is one like unto Him. Here is one surpassing in goodness. While this gaze is far beyond human comprehension, we can liken it to human experiences. Think, for instance, of a mother's gaze on her son. Regardless of how lovely the boy is by comparison to other boys, a mother typically loves her son the most. Why is that? In part, it is because he is hers. It is not that the mother is an egotist, concerned only with herself and her own. Rather, it is that, as his mother, she recognizes the loveliness of her son and loves him in turn. Likeness begets love. Returning to Saint Augustine's analogy, we see that the realization of a like goodness is expressed in an ecstasy—a going out—of love. Love breaks forth eternally from the relationship of Father and Son with a spontaneity and fruitfulness proper to God alone.

This Love springing forth from Father and Son is itself so perfect as to be another Person. Like the Father's act of knowing, the Father's and Son's act of loving is so rich, so potent, containing in itself the whole being of God, that it too bursts with life, a life born of the love of Father and Son. This impulse of love breathed forth from on high is a living self, one who is equally God with the Father and Son. He is, of course, the Holy Spirit.

If we want to sum all of this up in a few words, our Lord Himself gives us a quick description of the mystery. It takes all of five words to say: "The Father loves the Son"

(Jn 5:20). There, in those five words, we have a thumbnail sketch of the divine life. The Father loves the Son, His perfect likeness. That love is a Person, the Holy Spirit.

To say that we are made to share in the divine life means that we are made to share in the very relations of Father, Son, and Holy Spirit. In the Christian life and in the Christian liturgy, we assume the place of Christ in the Blessed Trinity to partake of His Sonship in the Spirit. In Christ, we get the Father. In Christ, we get the Spirit. The Son took flesh to insert us into this communion. As Saint Thomas Aquinas writes in the *Office of Corpus Christi*: "Since it was the will of God's only-begotten Son that men should share in his divinity, he assumed our nature in order that by becoming man he might make men gods."[5]

The sacraments, and in a special way the Holy Mass, grant us entry into the life of the Trinity. We may not often think about it, but the liturgy is a Trinitarian prayer. It is offered *to* the Father, *through* the Son, and *in* the Spirit. (It is also offered *by* Christ, but more on that later.) In the *General Instruction of the Roman Missal* we read, "The Priest calls upon the people to lift up their hearts toward the Lord in prayer and thanksgiving; he associates the people with himself in the Prayer that he addresses in the name of the entire community to God the Father through Jesus Christ in the Holy Spirit."[6] So, too, we see this Trinitarian stamp in the very structure of the liturgy's prayers. To take one example, the Collect for the Fourth Sunday of Lent reads, "O God, who through your Word reconcile the human race to yourself in a wonderful way, grant, we pray, that

[5] Thomas Aquinas, *Opusculum 57 in festo Corporis Christi*, lect. 1–4, in *The Liturgy of the Hours*, vol. 3, trans. ICEL, Office of Readings for the Solemnity of Corpus Christi (New York: Catholic Book Publishing, 1975), 610.

[6] "General Instruction of the Roman Missal", in *The Roman Missal*, 3rd ed., trans. ICEL (New Jersey: Catholic Book Publishing, 2011), §78.

with prompt devotion and eager faith the Christian people may hasten toward the solemn celebrations to come. Through our Lord Jesus Christ, your Son, who lives and reigns with you in the unity of the Holy Spirit, God, for ever and ever."

The liturgy reflects the Lord's intention for our deification. The ministry of the priest is so very meager, the prayers of the people so very modest. And yet, because it is truly Christ's prayer to the Father in the Spirit, the meager and modest become marvelous. At Mass, we take up Christ's place at the altar so as to assume His place in the Godhead. As we praise and adore, atone and sacrifice, plead and petition, the Incarnate Word pulls us out of the narrow limits of our humanity into the boundless glory of His divinity—into the very fullness of Trinitarian life.

## A Way to the Father

We can take some time, then, to elaborate on the Trinitarian relations that Christ opens to us through the liturgy. Let's start with Christ's relationship to the Father.

Some of you reading this book may not have the best relationship with your fathers, whether your biological father or the father of your parish. A father should evoke thoughts of provision, protection, love, and affirmation. Sadly, some of us can only recall ambivalence, neglect, or even abuse. Against the backdrop of a fraught or fatherless past, relating to God in this way may be hard. And yet, God reveals Himself in these terms. Why?

There is something in us that needs a father's love, a love that begets us, a love that is always present and always strong. We feel that, even if we do not have a father who loves us, *we ought to have one.* At times, the desire for a father's love can be a source of exasperation. Would it not be easier just to move on and secure ourselves against the risk of disappointment? But we cannot just move on or seal off that part of our heart. We are made for this relationship, and we cannot reach perfection, the fullness of our identity, without it.

It is notable that Christ—the pattern of our perfection—rarely speaks of Himself without reference to His Father. The Father is absolutely central to His ministry. In the whole Old Testament, God is called "father" only a handful of times; by contrast, in the Gospel of John alone, the Lord refers to the Father some one hundred and twenty times. If Christ had chosen to speak only one word for the whole of His earthly pilgrimage, it may very well have been: "Father!" He comes to reveal the Father: "No one knows the Son except the Father, and no one knows the Father except the Son and any one to whom the Son chooses to reveal him" (Mt 11:27). What is more, Christ offers us—in His person—a path to the Father whom He reveals: "I am the way, and the truth, and the life; no one comes to the Father, but by me" (Jn 14:6). Christ leads us along this path to partake of His intimate relationship with the Father.

Of course, Christ alone is the natural Son of God and the only-begotten of the Father. We do not usurp His place in the Trinity, nor do we divide His sonship among ourselves. Rather, we participate in His relationship to the Father as *adopted* sons and daughters; as Saint Paul writes, Jesus Christ is the "first-born of all creation" (Col 1:15). He is "Son" in the way that we are not and never can be; yet through the Father's gracious will, the "family" of God has expanded, so that we are heirs to the same inheritance that Christ enjoys as the natural Son (Eph 2:19). As adopted sons and daughters of God, we are adopted brothers and sisters of Christ.

This is the very stuff of our salvation and the whole of our religion. As Cardinal Jean Daniélou writes, "The heart and core of the irreducible originality of Christianity [is] that the Son of God came among us to reveal ... that there is within God himself a mysterious living love, called the Trinity of Persons; and that ... we men are called to share this life of love."[7] Christ alone gives us the power to be called children of the most high God.

## In the Spirit of Love

If Christ's sonship is the "what" of our salvation, the love of the Holy Spirit is the "how". The sacred authors continually link our share in Christ's Sonship to the gift of His Spirit. "By this we know that we abide in him and he in us, because he has given us of his own Spirit" (1 Jn 4:13). We are sons and daughters because Christ has given us the Holy Spirit, bestowing upon us the very love that unites Him to the Father. In the letter to the Romans, Saint Paul writes:

> [All] who are led by the Spirit of God are sons of God. For you did not receive the spirit of slavery to fall back into fear, but you have received the spirit of sonship. When we cry, "Abba! Father!" it is the Spirit himself bearing witness with our spirit that we are children of God, and if children, then heirs, heirs of God and fellow heirs with Christ. (Rom 8:14–17)

The word "heir" is quite strong. We have an established place in the household, a stable share in the inheritance. Our sonship is something to which we can *lay claim*. God has revealed His name so that we can call upon Him. The name used by sons—"Abba, Father!"—shows how far we have come from fear into security and the assurance of hope.

[7] Jean Daniélou, *The Lord of History: Reflections on the Inner Meaning of History*, trans. Nigel Abercrombie (London: Longmans, Green, 1958), 118.

This "spirit of sonship" is not some impersonal energy, like the Force. It is the Spirit Himself, dwelling in us and bringing in His very Person our inheritance: the Love between the Father and the Son. "God's love has been poured into our hearts through the Holy Spirit who has been given to us" (Rom 5:5). We play host to the Blessed Trinity and so delight in its ineffable life of love.

This is an essential part of the story of our becoming like Christ. The Spirit dwells in the Son in all His fullness. In Saint Luke's Gospel, Jesus is described as "full of the Holy Spirit" and "led by" Him (4:1), and Jesus Himself tells us that the "Spirit of the Lord" is upon Him (4:18). By receiving the Spirit, then, we share in the superabundant holiness of Jesus Christ. We enter into the innermost mystery of the Son's incarnate life, a life shaped by the love and praise of the Father. The Eucharist mediates this mystery to us. In filling the Eucharist with His own presence, the Son fills it also with His Spirit. As Saint Ephrem the Syrian writes, "He who eats it with faith, eats Fire and Spirit.... Take and eat this, all of you, and eat with it the Holy Spirit."[8] As we profess, Christ is present in the Blessed Sacrament in His body, blood, soul, and divinity. As His divine person breathes forth the Holy Spirit and His soul is filled with the grace of the Holy Spirit, so with each Holy Communion we receive the Holy Spirit in turn. As Matthias Scheeben writes:

> He [the Holy Spirit] lives on in the Son's flesh and blood with His fire and His vitalizing energy, as proceeding from the Son, and fills the sacred humanity with His own being to sanctify and glorify it. Particularly in the Eucharist He glorifies and spiritualizes the Son's human nature like a

[8] Ephrem the Syrian, *Sermo IV in Hebdomadam Sanctam*: CSCO 413/Syr. 182, 55. Quoted in John Paul II, *Ecclesia de Eucharistia* (April 17, 2003), §17.

> flaming coal, so that it takes on the qualities of sheer fire and pure spirit. Straightway He makes use of the Eucharist as an instrument to manifest His sanctifying and transforming power to all who come into contact with it, and as a channel to communicate Himself to all who receive it and feast upon it.[9]

In the Eucharist, the Spirit comes to dwell in us, to unite Himself to us, to consume us with His spiritual fire, to make us sons and daughters in the Son.

## You Are the Beloved

Through your baptism, you have "put on Christ" (Gal 3:27); this means that the words the Father speaks to His Son are now addressed *to you*. Christ's Baptism and Transfiguration illustrate this Trinitarian mystery with brilliant clarity. At the Baptism, the Spirit descends in the form of a dove as the voice of the Father booms out: "This is my beloved Son, with whom I am well pleased" (Mt 3:17). At the Transfiguration, the Spirit envelops Christ in the form of a cloud as the voice of the Father repeats the strain. "This is my beloved Son, with whom I am well pleased; listen to him" (Mt 17:5). In Christ, you behold your identity. In Christ, you behold your destiny. The Father loves the Son in the Spirit, and you partake of the life of the Son. Therefore the Father loves *you* in the Spirit, with a truly infinite delight and affection. As the Gospel of Luke has it: "*You* are my beloved Son; with *you* I am well pleased" (Lk 3:22; emphasis added).

[9] Matthias Joseph Scheeben, *The Mysteries of Christianity*, trans. Cyril Vollert, S.J. (St. Louis: B. Herder, 1946), 529.

The gift of divine love is always there for us. We do not need to strive to keep it "up and running". We can repose in it, for we are never in danger of losing the love of God. Of course, we can exclude ourselves from God's love for a time by sin. But when we do, God awaits us with open arms. More than that, He sees us from a distance, runs to us, and embraces us with His love at the slightest opportunity.

Recognize and receive this truth. Let it call forth acts of faith, hope, and love. You are not in danger of losing the love of God. "I am sure that neither death, nor life, nor angels, nor principalities, nor things present, nor things to come, nor powers, nor height, nor depth, nor anything else in all creation, will be able to separate us from the love of God in Christ Jesus our Lord" (Rom 8:38–39). You can trust this love forever. You can lean on it.

We can see glimmers of this kind of love in our human relationships. Perhaps the strongest example for many of us is the love of our mothers. That is certainly the case for me. I was not the worst of kids, but I still caused my mom plenty of grief. I broke more household goods than I can count, disobeyed my fair share of direct requests or commands, and arrived home after curfew on countless occasions. In the heat of the moment, my mother would let me know that she was upset, but at no point in my childhood did I worry that she would love me less. I knew beyond a shadow of a doubt that my mom loved me, that she would always love me. The love of a mother is unconditional and powerful. (In difficult situations, I often think of my mom because I need to recall that my life is built on solid love.) But even the love of a mother absolutely pales in comparison with the love of God. "Can a mother forget her infant, be without tenderness for the child of her womb? Even should she forget, I will never forget you" (Is 49:15 [NABRE]).

The unwavering love of God is the truth at the root of who you are. What does it matter what happens? The

Father loves you as He loves the Son, for, in truth, you are His son! You are His daughter! This relationship can bear all things, believe all things, hope all things, endure all things. This relationship never fails (see 1 Cor 13:7).

## Hidden with Christ in God

In order to live out our identity as the Beloved, however, we need to look constantly to the One in whom we receive that identity: Jesus Christ. He is not just a convenient way or an efficient way into the life of God. Christ is the *only* way into the life of God, and we are sons and daughters to the degree that we follow after Him. As Dietrich von Hildebrand writes, "Only the God-man, Jesus Christ, can truly offer adoration and love to God.... The final, supernatural vocation of every man is, therefore, transformation in Christ ... we can become holy only to the extent that we cease to live, and Christ lives in us."[10] If we are going to live for the Father, we have to get out of our own way and open a space in which Christ can unfold His own life in us. We cannot go on just living our little lives. We need to live *His* life. We need to be transformed, to be transfigured.

This is what the Christian tradition means when it speaks of "dying to self": I am no longer the center of my own life. God is. I must be displaced from the center of my own thought and affection if Christ is to occupy this place, His rightful place. "I have been crucified with Christ; it is no longer I who live, but Christ who lives in me; and the life I now live in the flesh I live by faith in the Son of God, who loved me and gave himself for me" (Gal 2:20). We are meant to be swept up into the identity of

[10] Dietrich von Hildebrand, *Liturgy and Personality* (Steubenville: Hildebrand Project, 2016), 10.

the Son, the perfect Image of the Father. Christ desires to live His life again in each of us. And the more we grow in holiness, the more this desire becomes our own.

In one of her most beautiful prayers, Saint Elizabeth of the Trinity, a young Carmelite, perfectly sums up all we have been discussing:

> O my God, Trinity whom I adore, help me to forget myself entirely that I may be established in You as still and as peaceful as if my soul were already in eternity....
>
> O my beloved Christ ... identify my soul with all the movements of Your Soul, to overwhelm me, to possess me, to substitute Yourself for me that my life may be but a radiance of Your Life....
>
> O consuming Fire, Spirit of Love, "come upon me," and create in my soul a kind of incarnation of the Word: that I may be another humanity for Him in which He can renew His whole Mystery. And You, O Father, bend lovingly over Your poor little creature;... seeing in her only the "Beloved in whom You are well pleased."
>
> O my Three, my All, my Beatitude, infinite Solitude, Immensity in which I lose myself, I surrender myself to You as Your prey. Bury Yourself in me that I may bury myself in You until I depart to contemplate in Your light the abyss of Your greatness.[11]

Saint Elizabeth's prayer gives expression to our highest ambition. We want to banish all distance between us and God. We want to think the same thoughts and love the same things. We want to be caught up in His very life.

If all of this sounds a little scary, a little radical, that is okay. You need not fear. God will not crush you. He will not destroy you. At times it sounds like the exaltation of

[11] Elizabeth of the Trinity, "I Have Found God", in *The Complete Works*, vol. 1, *General Introduction, Major Spiritual Writings*, trans. Aletheia Kane, O.C.D. (Washington, D.C.: ICS Publications, 1984), 183–84.

Christ means the extinction of your personality, that bringing Christ to the foreground means the extinction of everything that makes you "you". But just the opposite is true. For we do not even know who we are until Christ reveals us to ourselves, and the one who made your personality certainly knows how to perfect it. You will change: the excesses and defects of your character will be evened out. Things that you thought were important may fade away. But your true identity will take fuller and fuller shape.

This is the paradox of our faith: only by dying to ourselves and living to God in Christ can we come into possession of our identity. And there is no substitute for making that act of trust, that act of surrender. An oft-quoted line from *Gaudium et Spes* tells us that, "Only in the mystery of the incarnate Word does the mystery of man take on light.... Christ, the final Adam, by the revelation of the mystery of the Father and His love, fully reveals man to man himself and makes his supreme calling clear."[12] If we care to know who we are and what we are for, we have to be hidden in Christ. "For you have died, and your life is hidden with Christ in God" (Col 3:3). In Him lies concealed the love of Father, Son, and Holy Spirit—the love for which we are made.

## Holding the Gaze of Christ

The heights we have surveyed can be dizzying, so I want to end our discussion of the divine life with a final note of encouragement. Servant of God Luigi Giussani once observed that when you hold the gaze of the beloved, all is made right. You might have a thousand anxieties on your mind, but there is peace—or the beginning of peace—in the sight

[12] Second Vatican Council, *Gaudium et Spes* (December 7, 1965), §22.

of the beloved. You might be driven mad by sadness or anger, but it is all made lighter before the beholding of one who cares. The beloved communicates a simple affirmation: It is good that you exist. So, too, an aspiration: I want to be with you. In these truths, we each find strength to endure.

That is why the sacred liturgy occupies such a central place in our lives. Dietrich von Hildebrand writes that "[in the liturgy] Christ eternally turns His Face both toward the Father *and* toward us."[13] From the altar, Christ gazes into the depths of our soul. He sees and calls forth in us what we cannot see or muster in ourselves: a capacity for worship and communion. He asks only that we hold His gaze in turn, looking neither to another nor to ourselves. Clinging to Christ, we assume His place within the Blessed Trinity. Our meager and modest love is inflamed by contact with the love of Father, Son, and Holy Spirit.

We will never have the gift of our divine life "figured out"—we can no more take in the full mystery of God than we can put the ocean in a coffee mug. Even in heaven, we will not fully comprehend God. "[F]or God is greater than our hearts" (1 Jn 3:20). Nevertheless, Christ does not ask us to perform an impossible task. If we can but hold the gaze of Christ, all will be made right. "[For] we all, with unveiled face, beholding the glory of the Lord, are being changed into his likeness from one degree of glory to another" (2 Cor 3:18).

This helps us to simplify our expectations in life. Christ will make His plans for us known in His time and in His way. In the meantime and in eternity, we can expect Christ. He will be faithful, He will draw near, He will make us like Himself.

[13] Von Hildebrand, *Liturgy and Personality*, 118.

# Chapter 3

# Establishing Contact

Having a lofty goal can be inspiring and ennobling. It gets you out of bed in the morning. It prompts hard work. It keeps you from settling. And yet, the goal itself is not magic. It does not always motivate. At times, it can dispirit, discourage, or even paralyze us. When it seems so far off, the grandeur of the aim becomes a source of sadness and a judgment on our countless failures along the way. "How did I ever think this was possible?" "Why did I even bother when I was bound to fail?"

I was recently assigned to pursue a doctorate. The goal was to write a dissertation. At the outset, I was more than a little nervous. The subject was vast, my insights were slight, and time was ticking. But I knew that, my own temperamental disobedience notwithstanding, I had signed up for a life of obedience. So, I got to work. I compiled a bibliography, worked through books and articles, typed up notes, and refined my outlines. Before I knew it, I had finished the first chapter, albeit with a good deal of whining and complaining. The other chapters followed. Along the way, there were lots of emotional ups and downs. But, by chipping away day in and day out, my moods evened out, and eventually I had something to turn in. Throughout the process, I grew in the conviction that it *could* be done and *would* be done. I only needed to remain constant and take the steps that lay between me and the journey's end.

As we have seen, Christians have the most sublime goal imaginable—the very life of God. Christ Himself welcomes us into the communion of Father, Son, and Holy Spirit. It almost boggles the mind. How are we supposed to live like this? How are we supposed to share in God's very life? Seeking sanctity is not for the faint of heart, and the danger of despair is real. As with anything in life, though, the key is to remain firm in our purpose and to use the gifts that God gives us.

In the last chapter, we identified the most perfect of these gifts—our Lord Himself. Uniting in His person both divinity (which is our goal) and humanity (which is our starting point), Christ gets us where we need to go. He promises us Himself and gives us Himself; He is totally "for" us. We have only to hold His gaze. This helps us to set our expectations and resist the temptation to lose heart.

But there is more to be said. We need a clear plan, with straightforward action steps. In this chapter, we will look at the means, the concrete helps, that God supplies for arriving at our exalted end. That is, we will explore how exactly we get "plugged into" the saving power of the God-man, Jesus Christ. In what follows, we will lay out three of these means: first, the mysteries of the Son's incarnate life, His sufferings and deeds; second, the gift of faith, which puts us in spiritual contact with these mysteries and shapes us in their image; and third, the sacraments, which put us in bodily contact with God's power at work in the life of Christ.

## The Pioneer and Perfecter of Our Faith

Most of us, if asked how Jesus saves, would point to the Cross—and rightly so. But there is more to the story than that.

We have already spelled out the basic "logic" of the Incarnation, and you have no doubt heard it a thousand times: God the Son lives our human life so that we can live His divine life. Yet how often do we pause actually to think through the details of this statement? Christ *lives our life*. He puts our humanity through its saving paces in His own person. In doing so, He fills each dimension of our human life with His divine grace. He sketches the plan for us, works out its details, and provides the action steps. The thirty-three years that Christ spent on earth are His concrete proposal for our salvation.

This means that Christ's life in the flesh transforms every part of our human nature, which He took on whole and entire. He assumed a human soul and a human body, a human intellect and a human will. He assumed even human emotions and the defects and punishments associated with human sin. Christ thinks like us, chooses like us, and feels like us; He hungers and thirsts, suffers and dies like us. Every part of our nature has a place in Him, a meaning in Him, a purpose in Him.

Furthermore, He sanctifies every stage, activity, and experience of an ordinary human life. He was conceived, born, and grew up in a family; He learned a trade and worked at it; He was baptized and encountered temptation; He made friends and enemies; He suffered hostility, ridicule, and even slander; He knew the heartbreak of betrayal, the pain of abandonment—and in a most supreme way, He knew the truth of the triumph of love over evil. Every part of our story is taken up in Christ's human life.

Because He is God in the flesh, each of Christ's acts is sufficient for the salvation of the whole world; indeed, the very smallest of His deeds and sufferings are *more* than sufficient. As Saint Thomas Aquinas writes in the hymn *Adoro te devote*: "Jesus, Lord! Cleanse me, unclean as I am, with your blood, one drop of which can save the whole world from every sin."[1] Christ could easily have taken human flesh, performed one charitable and meritorious act, and then returned to heaven with His plans accomplished. So, why does He go through a decades-long earthly pilgrimage? In short, He does it for love!

Christ did not come to make a deal or settle a score by giving the bare minimum. He did not come to buy us back with *enough* of His blood. Rather, He came to bestow the depth and breadth of God's love for us in the most excellent and extravagant fashion. So great is His desire to be near us that He personally enters into every dimension of our human lives, transfiguring them with His love and enabling our own response of love. The mysteries of the life of Jesus Christ are God's various repetitions and rewordings, the various embellishments and emphases of His infinite love touching upon all of the different details of our human existence. Christ's life is like a beautiful and intricate piece of music, played to catch our ear and so to draw us into the beauty and simplicity of God. The events of Christ's life are but variations on a theme, the theme of God's love for us.

The mysteries of Christ's life are privileged places of encounter with the love of God. They are not museum pieces restricted to their historical setting, but living realities at work in the here and now. In every generation, they work to "sync" our lives with that of Christ. Christ continues to touch our lives with the grace of His Passion, thereby putting sin to death in our members. "We know that our former man was crucified with him so that the

[1] Thomas Aquinas, *Adoro te devote*: "Pie pellicane Iesu Domine | Me immundum munda tuo Sanguine | Cuius una stilla salvum facere | Totum mundum quit ab omni scelere." (Translation mine.)

sinful body might be destroyed, and we might no longer be enslaved to sin" (Rom 6:6). Christ continues to touch our lives with the grace of His Resurrection unto newness of life. "But if we have died with Christ, we believe that we shall also live with him" (Rom 6:8). The liturgy facilitates this transformation by putting us in touch with the mysteries. As Romano Guardini writes, "[T]he liturgy is no mere commemoration of what once existed, but is living and real; it is the enduring life of Jesus Christ in us, and that of the believer in Christ, eternally God and Man."[2] In fact, all of the liturgies and devotions of the Christian life really have this one goal: to harmonize the "music" of our own lives with that of Christ, so that "Christ plays in ten thousand places, | Lovely in limbs, and lovely in eyes not his | To the Father through the features of men's faces."[3]

To take a particularly clear example, we can think about the holy Rosary, in which we pray to "imitate what [the mysteries] contain" and "obtain what they promise". Many people see the Rosary as a kind of meditative chore. Am I supposed to think about the words I am reciting or the mysteries I am recalling or the God I am addressing? The answer is, yes! But do not worry too much about holding it all together. Through grace, Christ is at work in your life; so too are His mysteries. His Baptism, temptation, and public life; His Passion, death, and Resurrection; His every deed and suffering are at work in your life. When praying the Rosary, we simply try to further this work by recalling the various deeds and sufferings in which Christ demonstrates His love for us. This "spiritual contact" serves to deepen our conversion and quicken our

[2] Romano Guardini, *The Spirit of the Liturgy*, trans. Ada Lane (New York: Crossroad, 1998), 50.

[3] Gerard Manley Hopkins, "As Kingfishers Catch Fire", in *Poems of Gerard Manley Hopkins*, ed. Robert Bridges (Oxford: Oxford University Press, 1948), 95.

love for Him. We can then cleave to God more firmly as we live our own baptisms, temptations, and public ministries, our own passions, deaths, and resurrections. We can become Christlike, seeking faithfully the will of the Father. By attending to His mysteries in prayer, in the sacred liturgy, and beyond, we "imitate" and "obtain" the very life of Christ.

## Access by Faith

You might still be wondering, at this point, how it makes any sense to speak of real "contact" with the deeds and sufferings of Christ's life. After all, we believe that Jesus Christ lived on earth some two thousand years ago. The answer is *faith*. Many people think of faith as something vague, something wispy or fluffy—certainly not capable of providing something so solid as contact. But faith gives us an intellectual "grasp" on reality. It affords us a genuine insight by imparting a "God's-eye-view" and broadening the scope of the world in which we live.

To unpack this, we can think about some examples of natural faith. We believe that Moscow is where the cartographer plots it. We believe that the molecular structure of benzene is how the chemist models it. We believe that our parents are, in fact, who they say they are. There are certain things that we do not observe or cannot observe. They might be too small, too far away, or just too hard to gauge. In these circumstances, we consult experts or privileged observers, who put us in contact with what they know. Provided they are not deceived or deceitful, we take their testimony as true and move on with life.

Without this basic kind of faith, our lives would be a lot less real. Think about it. How do I know that the flight will land when and where the airline says it will? Perhaps it is best to drive the sixteen hours to *ensure* my arrival. Or how do I know that my friend really loves me? Perhaps it is best to remain a little distant lest he think me overly familiar. If I insist on verifying everything, if I am unable to function before removing the possibility of error, I shrink the world in which I am able to operate. Chronic unbelief keeps us from flourishing and robs us of a healthy experience of life.

And that is just with natural faith. The stakes are even higher in the realm of revelation. There are plenty of things that no one on earth can observe, and these just so happen to be the most important things of all. How do you know that God is who He says He is? How do you know that your sins are forgiven? How do you know that the bread and wine become the body and blood of Christ? Our only way of accessing these realities, of establishing contact with the deepest of mysteries, is by God's gift of supernatural faith.

Again, we tend to think of faith as something ephemeral. But the Letter to the Hebrews tells us that it "is the assurance of things hoped for, the conviction of things not seen" (Heb 11:1). Faith provides an intellectual "grip" that is firmer than anything we gain through human reason. Why? Because it is based on divine testimony. God speaks truly of Himself and His creation. The One who is all-knowing and all-good is neither deceived nor deceitful. Period. With the gift of faith, God gives us access to this testimony. Faith thus heightens our understanding and uncovers realities otherwise known only to God. Faith transforms our whole thought world. It both *heals* and *elevates*.

Sin wounds our minds, plunging us into patterns of unreality and irrationality, afflicting us with a kind of voluntary madness. "And men loved darkness rather than light, because their deeds were evil" (Jn 3:19). In this state, we become blind to the truth only to stumble and fall in the gloom of ignorance. Despite our obsession with science and our fascination with trivia, we prove unwilling to acquire saving knowledge. Whether by neglecting our study of the faith or inquiring curiously into the occult, we can debase our own thought world.

Faith saves us from this degradation. It heals our mental malady. You may have noticed in your relationships that you rarely get anywhere when you argue about controversial issues like abortion or transgenderism. Most people have their minds made up and are not willing to budge. Sometimes, though, you witness a miraculous change as the obstacles to open and honest conversation are simply removed. In my experience, this change often happens after someone receives (or prepares to receive) the gift of faith. Faith heals the mind. It repairs the damage done by sin and orients our thinking to its supernatural goal.

Faith also elevates us. It transports our minds to a higher plane. It gives us the capacity to understand what God has to say about Himself and to respond in turn. It puts us in conversation with God. As rational creatures, we have a share in God's own intelligence. Mind you, we are relatively simple creatures (with relatively simple minds), and so our share is rather weak. We can only perceive so much before we realize that we do not perceive everything. Faith expands our capacity for perception. At our creation, God has given us a share in His divine light. By the gift of faith, He gives us a fuller share, sharpening our minds and broadening our understanding. Faith helps us to grasp the things of nature with greater sensitivity and even to arrive at things beyond nature. As Saint Thomas Aquinas writes, "Before the coming of Christ, no philosopher, despite all his efforts, could know enough about God and the things necessary for eternal salvation, which, after the coming of Christ, even a little old lady knows by faith."[4] Faith, by its penetrating light, gives us richer access to the luminous mind of God Himself.

Although faith is and always remains a gift, it is truly ours to use—a power that we can exercise and that can mature in us. When we make acts of faith, we dispose ourselves to receive greater faith. There is a very simple action step here: *believe*, and ask for firmer belief (see Mk 9:24). Think of a hallway equipped with motion-sensor lights. You might hesitate to walk forward, protesting that you need more light to know where you are going. But it is only by taking one step and then another that you get more and more light to walk by. Similarly, when we take steps to nourish our life of faith through regular prayer, worthy reception of the sacraments, penance, study, solid friendships, and so forth, God proves Himself generous. As we mature in our belief and make repeated acts of faith, the light grows—we gain a keener sense for the things of God, obedience to His promptings, and an awareness of His presence and activity in our lives. Faith thus acclimatizes us to the life of heaven, preparing us for the beatific vision in which God will be all in all.

## The Shape of the Sacraments

We have seen how the mysteries of Christ's human life, and the virtue of faith by which we access those mysteries, put us in contact with Christ. Our final task for the chapter

[4] Thomas Aquinas, *In symbolum apostolorum*, prol.: "... nullus philosophorum ante adventum Christi cum toto conatu suo potuit tantum scire de Deo et de necessariis ad vitam aeternam, quantum post adventum Christi scit una vetula per fidem." (Translation mine.)

is to continue on with the sacraments. The sacraments extend the logic of the Incarnation into the materiality of our human existence. The language, gestures, and rituals of the sacraments effectively apply Christ's life—his Baptism, temptation, and public ministry; His Passion, death, and Resurrection—to ours. They wash us, renew us, and feed us; and, in doing so, they unleash the graces with which Christ infused His earthly existence.

In the Gospel account of Jesus' Baptism, we can discern something of His saving purpose at work in the sacramental economy. Recall that Christ is utterly sinless and full of grace. Baptism, for Him, is not a matter of necessity. He does not need to be cleansed from sin or filled with divine life. Saint John the Baptist acknowledges the fact: "John would have prevented him, saying, 'I need to be baptized by you, and do you come to me?' But Jesus answered him, 'Let it be so now; for thus it is fitting for us to fulfil all righteousness.' Then he consented" (Mt 3:14–15). Why, then, was Christ baptized?

As Saint Ambrose teaches, "Therefore, the Lord was baptized, not wanting to be cleansed but to cleanse the waters [so] that, purified by the flesh of Christ which knew not sin, they would have the power (*ius*) of baptism."[5] At His Baptism, Christ is imparting to the waters their very capacity to bear His grace. He thus forges the connection between His life and ours. Christ was baptized for *your* righteousness. He was baptized for *you*.

The sacraments do not bear a generic grace, they bear the graces of Christ's mysteries in the flesh. This relationship between the sacraments and the mysteries is particularly

[5] Ambrose of Milan, *Exposition of the Gospel According to Saint Luke*, bk. 2, lin. 1121: "Baptizatus ergo est Dominus non mundari uolens, sed mundare aquas, ut ablutae per carnem Christi, quae peccatum non cognouit, baptismatis ius haberent." (Translation mine.)

evident in the way the Scriptures speak of baptism. As Saint Paul explains, the liturgy of baptism concentrates the power of Christ's Passion and Resurrection and brings them to bear on the recipient: "Do you not know that all of us who have been baptized into Christ Jesus were baptized into his death? We were buried therefore with him by baptism into death, so that as Christ was raised from the dead by the glory of the Father, we too might walk in newness of life" (Rom 6:3–4). Through His baptism, each new Christian suffers with Christ, dies with Christ, and rises with Christ. The old man passes away. The new man comes to be. "You have put off the old man with his practices and have put on the new man, which is being renewed in knowledge" (Col 3:9–10).

Sacramental signs, thus, bear mysterious graces. Pause for a moment and think about the wisdom and mercy of this arrangement. Though burgeoning with divine power, the sacraments meet our human frailty with a gentle touch, employing the ordinary and the familiar to bless us. There is nothing dazzling about water and oil, bread and wine, or the particular words used in sacramental rites. Rather, the Lord "veils" His glory in humble signs, thus communicating His divine life to human beings without overwhelming or crushing us. In an uncomplicated, fifteen-minute ritual, Baptism brings about divine adoption. It does not require us to be smart. It does not even require us to be aware. It simply does what it signifies, uniting us to the Baptism of Christ and reclaiming us as sons of God.

Part of the simplicity (and appeal) of the sacraments arises from their nearness to our human experience. At each significant moment, we see beautiful parallels between natural and supernatural life. In our bodily life, we are born; in our spiritual life, we are baptized. In our bodily life, we mature to adulthood; in our spiritual life, we are confirmed. In our bodily life, we are nourished with food; in our spiritual life, we feed on the body and blood of Christ. Our bodily life is made orderly and fruitful; our spiritual life is blessed by priesthood and matrimony. In our bodily life, we are healed from illness; in our spiritual life, we are absolved and anointed. At each stage along the way, Christ is there to meet us in His mysteries, to meet us with His sacraments. This "mirroring" of biological events reminds us, again and again, that it is through the sacred humanity of Jesus Christ—and through it alone—that we receive the divine life. The sacraments mediate these mysteries. The sacraments pour out this grace.

## The Summit of Sacramental Life

Up to this point, we have emphasized what is common to "sacramentality" in general. But each of the sacraments channels the divine power in a unique way, capturing a different element of the divine plan and a different feature of Christ's life. This means that not all sacraments are "created equal". Rather, each occupies a place within a hierarchy, based on the role it plays in the story of salvation and the way it conforms us to Christ. One way to approach this question is by asking which sacrament is the "greatest". As it turns out, there are various ways to answer.

Baptism is, of course, the most necessary of sacraments. It opens to us the door of salvation and removes the greatest obstacle to divine life. Without Baptism, we risk dying in our sins. It also supplies an abundance of divine gifts—spiritual adoption, predestination to glory, and all manner of graces and virtues. As Saint Cyril of Jerusalem writes, "Great is the baptism being set before you. It is a release to prisoners, the forgiveness of sins, the death of sin, the regeneration of the soul, the putting on the garment of light, the indestructible holy seal, the chariot to heaven, the luxurious food of paradise, the gaining of the kingdom, and the grace of divine adoption."[6] Baptism lays the foundation for our sacramental existence and inaugurates our participation in the divine life.

For those who fall prey to post-baptismal sin, Penance is the most vital of sacraments. Without Penance, sinners risk remaining cut off from the graces they first knew at Baptism. As the author of the *Didache* writes, "Assemble on the Lord's Day, and break bread and offer the Eucharist; but first make confession of your faults, so that your sacrifice may be a pure one. Anyone who has a difference with his fellow is not to take part with you until they have been reconciled, so as to avoid any profanation of your sacrifice."[7] Penance reinstates us in *divine* life. How does it accomplish this? Well, it is no accident that the formula of absolution mentions the Lord's death, Resurrection, and sending of the Spirit. Through the words of the priest, the mysteries of Christ's life (and their attendant graces) are made mystically present. He heals us from past transgressions and elevates us to divine friendship. Each celebration of the sacrament brings about a new encounter with the Paschal Mystery through which Christ atoned for the sins of all mankind.

Without any qualification, though, the Eucharist is the greatest of the sacraments. As we read in the *Catechism*, "The Eucharist is 'the source and summit of the Christian life.' 'The other sacraments, and indeed all ecclesiastical ministries and works of the apostolate, are bound up with the

[6] Cyril of Jerusalem, Procatechesis 16, in *Lectures on the Christian Sacraments*, trans. Maxwell E. Johnson (Yonkers, N.Y.: St. Vladimir's Seminary Press, 2017).

[7] "The Didache" in *Early Christian Writings: The Apostolic Fathers*, trans. Maxwell Staniforth (New York: Penguin Books, 1987), 197.

Eucharist and are oriented toward it. For in the blessed Eucharist is contained the whole spiritual good of the Church, namely Christ himself, our Pasch'."[8] All of the sacraments look to the Eucharist. Baptism enables us to receive the Eucharist. Penance readmits us to the Eucharist. Holy Orders ensures that the Eucharist is celebrated. Several sacraments are celebrated in the setting of the Eucharistic liturgy.

Ecclesial life, our life, has a Eucharistic shape. Through faith and the sacraments, Christ leads us to the altar, and here we have another clear action step in our journey into the divine life: receive His body and blood, and do it often and well. As Lawrence Feingold writes, "The Eucharist ... is the principal channel for the increase and nourishing of grace and charity, for that is its reason for being. The Eucharist was instituted precisely for this end. It is the sacrament of love and sanctification or 'divinization'."[9] In the Eucharist, we find our greatest help in living the life of grace and attaining to the life of God.

But that is not the only reason that the Eucharist is the greatest of the sacraments. There is a further and more important reason. The Eucharist makes God present in a *special* way. To understand how, we need to consider how the other sacraments make God present. "A sacrament", writes Saint Thomas Aquinas, "is a sign of a sacred thing that makes men holy."[10] The sacraments are signs that cause what they signify, and they signify salvation in one way or another. Compare this to the power of ordinary signs. Say you are driving along and you see a sign

[8] *CCC* 1324 (quoting *Lumen Gentium* 12 and *Presbyterorum Ordinis* 5).

[9] Lawrence Feingold, *The Eucharist: Mystery of Presence, Sacrifice, and Communion* (Steubenville: Emmaus Academic, 2018), 24.

[10] Thomas Aquinas, *Summa theologiae* IIIa q. 60, a. 2, resp.: "... ut scilicet proprie dicatur sacramentum ... quod est signum rei sacrae inquantum est sanctificans homines." (Translation mine.)

indicating your destination. You can choose to follow that sign or not. You might prefer to alter your itinerary. You might prefer to stop and get gas. You might do any number of things. A sacramental sign is far more powerful. If approached in faith, it causes what it signifies. It would be like a road sign that pulls you off the highway and delivers you safely to your destination.

We can therefore speak of the sacraments as "causes" of salvation. In Baptism, for example, the minister pours the water over the head of the recipient and pronounces the sacramental form: "Jocelyn, I baptize you in the name of the Father and of the Son and of the Holy Spirit." At that very moment, she is cleansed from sin and filled with grace. Provided there are not any obstacles in the way, she is—then and there—transformed by the sacrament. She receives the grace of adoption and becomes a child of God. Something analogous holds true for each of the sacraments. Christ is present in their power, a power unleashed by their respective signs. In their ritual action, the sacraments make Christ present *sacramentally* (shocking, I know).

We are now in a position to appreciate the special presence of the Eucharist. Like the other sacraments, the Eucharist makes Christ present *sacramentally*, by the power of its signs. But, the first thing that the Eucharist signifies just *is* Christ's body and blood: "This is my body.... This is my blood." At Mass, the substances of bread and wine become the substances of the body and blood of Our Lord Jesus Christ. So whereas the power of the other sacraments flows through their rites, the power of this sacrament pools up on the altar in the presence of the faithful. Water does not cease to be water because it is used in the baptismal rite. But bread and wine *do* cease to be bread and wine at the words of consecration and become, instead, our Lord Himself. The Eucharist, then, makes Christ present *substantially*.

We refer to this mystery as *transubstantiation*, which means a change in substance. To grasp this, we will need to take a quick crash course in philosophy. A "substance" names a "kind" of thing: rocks, plants, animals, human beings are all substances. A substance is something with coherence and integrity, something that acts for itself. We can clarify this idea by drawing a contrast with "accidents". Accidents, in philosophical terms, are like properties or attributes: Quantity, quality, time, and place are all accidents. An accident typically exists *in* a substance. Tallness, knowledge, and sonship are all accidents. So while you do not run into "tallness" or "blondness" walking around, you *do* run into tall, blond men.

Ordinarily, when something changes from one kind of thing to another kind of thing, from one substance to another, there is an accompanying change in appearance or "accidents". When you burn a log, it changes from brown to gray, from woody to ashy. When you kill a weed, it goes from green to brown, from supple to brittle. In the Eucharistic change, "ordinarily" does not apply. Bread and wine *become* Christ's body and blood, with no perceptible alteration to the matter. They still look like bread and wine.

In the Eucharistic change, what we have is a change in substance with no accompanying change in accidents. The elements look like bread and wine before the change, and they look like bread and wine after the change. But whereas formerly they were bread and wine, now they are the body and blood of Christ. To get somewhat technical for a moment, the accidents of bread and wine are miraculously suspended by God. They are no longer the accidents of this or that substance. They are no longer the properties or attributes of *anything*. God holds them in place to help us locate and believe in His body and blood. The sacrament of the Eucharist provides for our earthly natures, giving our senses something to "hold onto" as we are called up into heavenly realities.

To be clear, transubstantiation does not mean that the Lord transports Himself to the altar. Since the day of His Ascension, Jesus Christ is in one place and one place only—heaven, where He reigns in glory. Jesus is not flying around from country to country like a sort of sacramental Santa Claus, presenting Himself on each altar at the moment of the Consecration. There is a different kind of presence at work.

As we have said, the offering of the Mass makes Jesus Christ present *substantially*. The bread becomes the body of Christ *in the whole of His substance*, though not *in the same proportions* as His human body. This means that the dimensions of the sacramental bread are not changed into the dimensions of His glorified body. So, let's say Christ measures 5′11″ and weighs 165 pounds in heaven. It does not follow that each host will measure 5′11″ or weigh 165 pounds. We do not need that kind of change. It is not necessary for the conferral of grace. Note, Christ simply says, "This is my body." He does not add, "And it is going to look and feel exactly like my body." In pronouncing these words, Christ effects a change and institutes a sacrament. We have to grapple with that change and receive that sacrament, even if it boggles our minds a bit. In brief, His body is truly present, really present, under the appearance of bread, but it is present by way of substance, not by way of place or quantity or physical dimensions; the host does not assume the same proportions as His human body.

This introduces a further mode of Christ's presence. In the case of the Eucharistic bread, the body is there by the power of the sacrament. He said this is His body, and so it is. The sacrament signifies the change and causes the change. The blood, soul, and divinity are there by another mode of presence, by what we call natural or real *concomitance*. In heaven, Christ's body, blood, soul, and divinity are all together. In the Eucharistic change, the bread becomes His glorified body. Since His glorified body in heaven exists together with His blood, soul, and divinity, it follows that His Eucharistic body brings with it His blood, soul, and divinity. So even when you only receive the host, you receive His body *and* his blood, soul, and divinity. When you receive, whether under the appearance of bread or under the appearance of wine, you get all of Him.

What is the benefit of such abstruse theologizing? The implications of this teaching are simple but profound. In the Eucharist, Christ gives you *Himself*, whole and entire. He is present to you. He holds nothing of Himself back. Just as Christ supplied miraculously and abundantly for the wedding guests at the beginning of His public ministry—performing the task of the bridegroom for His bride—so in these latter days, He provides for us, the guests at His feast, in miraculous and abundant fashion. God provides Himself as food and drink for the banquet of salvation.[11]

The Eucharist gives us Christ in a way that surpasses every other sacrament. Here, we have another action step: *abide*. Christ has chosen to be with you. The Eucharist offers you a concrete way of being with Him—at Mass, in Adoration, in a life centered on Eucharistic worship. We hear from Christ's own lips, "He who eats my flesh and drinks my blood *abides in me and I in him*" (Jn 6:56; italics added).

The Eucharist shows most fantastically how far Christ will go in bestowing this love. Not only does He take our

[11] Brant Pitre, *Jesus the Bridegroom: The Greatest Love Story Ever Told* (New York: Image, 2018).

nature and live our life, He also prolongs His presence among us in most concrete fashion. In the Blessed Sacrament, Christ abides with us, remains with us. Matthias Scheeben writes:

> The changing of the bread into the body of Christ by the power of the Holy Spirit is a renewal of the wonderful act by which, in the power of the same Holy Spirit, He originally formed His body in the womb of the Virgin and took it to His person. As He effected His first entrance into the world by this act, so by that other act He multiplies His substantial presence over and over again in space and time. But this presence is multiplied only that the body of Christ may grow and spread throughout the members which He attaches to Himself and fuses with Himself.[12]

We are made to be joined to Him, to be "fused" with Him. We are made to become Him. The mysteries of His life effect this transformation even as the Eucharist provides the daily bread with which to endeavor the task. By attending to His mysteries in prayer, in the sacred liturgy, and beyond, we are "fused" with Christ. Here, we gain insight into our most basic questions: "Lord, who are you, and who am I?" By abiding with Him in faith, by gazing upon sacred signs and gaining access to sacred realities, we come to know God and come to find ourselves.

Having laid out some of the "technicalities" of Eucharistic theology, in the remaining chapters, we will be able to consider more closely the logic of our Eucharistic identity as it is played out in the signs of the liturgy. We are meant to be like God, to share in the communion of Father, Son, and Holy Spirit. This is the goal toward

[12] Matthias Joseph Scheeben, *The Mysteries of Christianity*, trans. Cyril Vollert, S.J. (St. Louis: B. Herder, 1946), 485–86.

which our earthly life progresses. The Lord institutes the sacrament of the Eucharist to bring about the transformation. By approaching in faith and receiving in sacrament, we get Him, and He makes us like Himself. God has set a lofty goal for us, but we need not despair. He supplies the means to secure it.

## Chapter 4

# Reading the Signs

We often describe the life of faith as a pilgrimage. As Christians, we are trying to reach a specific destination, and each day we have the opportunity to make a little progress toward it. A road may be long and tiresome, but if the destination is worthwhile, we are willing to put in the effort.

Let's say we decide to make a pilgrimage to a holy city, like Santiago de Compostela. This decision prompts a whole host of practical considerations: How many hours should we walk today? Where will we stop for food? Where will we spend the night? Fortunately, this is a well-traveled route. There are signs along the way that provide us the answers we need, pointing out landmarks, hostels, and restaurants with their different locations and distances. Relying on these signs, we determine the overall shape of the journey and make our way toward the destination. If we are wise travelers, we will take extra care to look for and heed those signs. Otherwise, we risk heading off-course, wandering aimlessly, or getting lost.

In the life of faith, we set out, not just toward any holy city, but to *the* holy city—the heavenly Jerusalem, where we hope to enjoy the very vision of God. Because the Lord desires our arrival, He provides abundantly for us in the pilgrimage that is the life of faith. The Scriptures, the Tradition, the Church's authority reveal the way to the holy city. The preaching and teaching of the Church's pastors, the witness of the saints, and the fellowship of the Christian community accompany us on the way.

Most importantly, the sacraments constitute sacred signs that orient our efforts and give us the grace we need to advance. As we saw in the previous chapter, the sacraments are not just any old signs. They do more than "instruct", as though merely "pointing out" landmarks, hostels, and restaurants to which we must make our own way. If received in faith, they give life, restore health, and nourish our spirits, conducting us safely along our pilgrim journey to the heavenly Jerusalem. In short, these are signs that promise to give us God.

We may not be especially good at reading these signs at the beginning of our journey or even at our present stage. That is okay. Just as the many miles along the pilgrim way tighten our muscles and toughen our feet, so a life of simple fidelity—oriented by sacramental signs—sharpens the mind and enlarges the heart of the Eucharistic wayfarer. As we get closer to the destination, we can expect both a deeper relationship with God and a deeper understanding of ourselves. For, in approaching the vision of God, we catch sight of who we are in His eyes.

## Setting an Intention

What does this fidelity look like, concretely? Is it a matter of squinting, straining, or thinking really hard? Weak as we are, it would be unsettling if our spiritual progress depended wholly on our own mental efforts and conscious choices. Well, you will be happy to learn that Saint Thomas Aquinas addresses this question and provides some consoling words. When it comes to reading the signs, he says, we need only *intend* and *attend*.

All human endeavors begin with formulating an intention. An intention expresses a resolve to pursue some goal: "I'm going to brew my own beer!" "I'm going to found a nonprofit!" "I'm going to become Catholic!" The intention gathers up our energy, moving us to make plans and take action steps. If we are going to get down to brass tacks in life, we have to be committed to an overall project that gives shape to the details.

Our life of faith—our life of Eucharistic worship—begins with this same kind of intention. With stakes that high, though, you might object: "I do not know if I can trust myself to formulate an intention. I have been so indecisive and inconstant in the past. Who is to say I will not continue to be so? Why intend something so noble when I am so silly and sinful?" Of course, we have all failed to follow through on our intentions—whether with diets, exercise routines, or prayer regimens. But, frankly, who cares? The definitive thing is that in the midst of our indecisiveness and inconstancy, God shows Himself faithful. He desires your salvation far more than you ever could. As Saint John Paul II once preached, "We are not the sum of our weaknesses and failures; we are the sum of the Father's love for us and our real capacity to become the image of his Son."[1] Thus, God delights in your every attempt to live a sacramental life. He welcomes your efforts and encourages them, however small.

In the life of prayer, then, merit depends primarily on intention. If we intend to pray and do what we can to safeguard that intention, God rewards our efforts. You may be distracted or fatigued, but if you do what lies within your power to be present, God will hear you graciously. If you say, for instance, "I would like to pray a Eucharistic

[1]John Paul II, Mass for the Celebration of the 17th World Youth Day in Downsview Park, Toronto: Homily (July 28, 2002), §5.

holy hour!" and get yourself to the adoration chapel, God blesses your intention. During that hour, you might spend a good part of the time thinking about dinner or even dozing off, but you need not worry too much. What counts is that you try, and ask for the grace to do better the next time. Perhaps you should listen to less music. Perhaps you should get more sleep. Your intention may need to be purified, but you can trust that God will see to that in due course. "Therefore do not be anxious about tomorrow, for tomorrow will be anxious for itself. Let the day's own trouble be sufficient for the day" (Mt 6:34).

At this point, you may raise another objection: "Should I not wait until I am on firmer footing? I am just recovering from a terrible relationship. I need to grow in my resolve before formulating an intention." Right? Wrong. The only way to begin is to begin. We all need to heal. We all need to grow. Formulating an intention for a life of Eucharistic worship is the source of that healing and growth. When you intend to arrive at the destination, you make an act of trust in God that He will conduct you hence. Sure, you are weak and wounded. We all are. But our weaknesses and wounds, if given over to Christ, can become a privileged place of encounter with *God's intention* for our salvation.

If you fear that your word is wobbly, Christ invites you to lay claim to His Word. As it turns out, you can just borrow His *intention*. "[God] desires all men to be saved and to come to the knowledge of the truth" (1 Tim 2:4). Christ has designs for your life. He has a plan for welfare and not for woe. He wants to share this plan with you, regardless of how fully you understand or desire it. He wants to give you the grace to carry it out. By laying claim to Christ's intention, we build our house upon solid rock. "And the rain fell, and the floods came, and the winds blew and beat upon that house, but it did not fall" (Mt 7:25).

How, then, do I formulate this intention? What about something like this: "Lord Jesus Christ, I want you, whole and entire. I want to live a life of Eucharistic worship. I do not want anything less than that fullness. I just want you. I want to be caught up in your life and in your plans for mine. I want to live your sacred mysteries in my own soul and body. I know this will be painful, but I am willing. I know I will have to confront my various sins and vices. That scares me. Please help me. Help me to be honest about my struggles. Help me to be steadfast in my resolve. Help me to be humble in my need. I know that I am lukewarm and overly comfortable. I hate this about myself, but I do not know how to change. Help me to be aware of my attachments. Help me to be zealous for your life. Help me to be radical in my conversion. I know this will mean dealing with ups and downs. I wish I could live a life of continual progress, but I doubt that I will. Help me not to indulge in sadness or anger when difficulties arise. Help me not to give way to despair. Help me not to put off my conversion until tomorrow, when I can endeavor it in simple ways today. Lord Jesus Christ, I want you, but apart from you I can do nothing. Grant me the grace to desire you more. Grant me the grace to pursue you well." Or something like that. Take time, write it down, return to it frequently in thought and in prayer. The God who has begun a good work in you will see it to completion (see Phil 1:6).

## Paying Attention

Intention gets us going in the right direction on our pilgrimage of Eucharistic worship, but there are still many steps to be taken along the way. Against the horizon of our *intention*, the Lord seeks to capture our *attention* as well.

Attention means something like caring about or referring ourselves to an object of thought and affection. It means looking for the signs and reading them well.

Attention makes us sensitive to what is meaningful and purposeful in life. It helps us connect the dots between our present experiences and their ultimate import. To be attentive means to remain curious about our experiences, to inquire after their meaning. It opens us to God and to His promptings. Only by remaining attentive do we escape the fate of the wanderer who drifts through life "in a state of spiritual inertia, [contemplating] in an isolated way what approaches him".[2] Throughout our day, we seek to act out of our *habitual* intention for God as we call forth *actual* attention to His various works.

In the context of the sacred liturgy, Saint Thomas gives us a clear roadmap for becoming more attentive. He encourages us to progress through the words of the liturgy to the senses of the words and ultimately to the God who is at work in both the words and their senses.

First, says Saint Thomas, attend to the words. Words are the building blocks of human thought and the ordinary means we use to engage with concepts and things. In our lives of Eucharistic worship, God accommodates Himself to human understanding by using human words. These words help us conceive of what God is doing in our lives. In the Scriptures, for example, God constrains His glory within the limits of human speech so that we can glimpse something of His glory. Our minds cannot grasp God whole and entire, but they *can* ponder the things He tells us about Himself. The sacred liturgy uses the Scriptures and the prayers of the Mass to describe for us both

[2] Dietrich von Hildebrand, *Liturgy and Personality* (Steubenville: Hildebrand Project, 2016), 63.

the pilgrim way and the life of heaven so that we can be drawn into those mysteries. It is for us to tune in and take note. This means listening to the words proposed by the liturgy and proclaimed from the pulpit. Origen sums it up nicely: Just as we should not let crumbs of the Lord's body fall from the altar, neither should we let crumbs of the word fall from our notice.[3]

Next, says Saint Thomas, attend to the *sense* of the words. Words are more than mere vocalizations. They refer to people, places, things—all of which are part of the story of our salvation. The words put us in touch with realities. When it comes to the sacred liturgy, it is not just a matter of memorizing our lines or remembering our cues. It is about following the words to the things they name, allowing our minds to be genuinely led by them. Yes, it is fruitful to say the prayers correctly—not adding or changing words, or stretching a note too long—but those kinds of mechanics are just the beginning. The words must become transparent to the very mysteries themselves, as we seek the Lord hidden by humble vesture.

That brings us to Saint Thomas' final point, which is that we must attend to *God Himself*. When we read the signs, taking in the words of the liturgy and their senses, we discover that all roads lead to God. God is the source and end of all creation. All things come from Him. All things are made for Him. All things can lift our minds and hearts to

[3] Origen, Homily 13.3 [on Exodus] in *Homilies on Genesis and Exodus*, trans. Ronald E. Heine (Washington, D.C.: Catholic University of America Press, 1982): "You who are accustomed to take part in divine mysteries know, when you receive the body of the Lord, how you protect it with all caution and veneration lest any small part fall from it, lest anything of the consecrated gift be lost.... But if you are so careful to preserve his body, and rightly so, how do you think that there is less guilt to have neglected God's word than to have neglected his body?"

Him. In an age of hustle and bustle, it can be tempting to look away from these indications, to push God to the periphery of our lives. We struggle to make God *fit* within our schedule. The liturgy—if we can quiet ourselves and let it do its work—retrains the mind to see God in all things and all things in God. If we are willing to be on pilgrimage, if we are willing to pay attention, we will find countless opportunities for communion. God has made us for Himself. He is present. We need only notice.

## Getting Out of the Way

In a surprising statement, Saint Thomas says that, of all the things that we have listed—words, senses, and God—it is easiest for us to pay attention to God. If we had to rank them in terms of their intelligibility, we would probably say the words, then the senses, and then God. But Saint Thomas insists that it is just the opposite. Using some strong language, he says that while words and senses can be difficult to grasp, even the least intelligent among us can attend to God.

The words and their senses are part of the pilgrimage, but they are not meant to be final destinations. If they are treated as such, they can even become obstacles. To obsess over a word might make you lose sight of the sentence. When reading in public, people will often overemphasize certain consonants or get confused over which syllable to stress. In these moments, we forget the point of the oration because its parts have become a distraction. The consonants and syllables ought to be in service of the words, the words of the sentences, and the sentences of the oration. Ultimately, the point of the words and their senses is to put us in touch with reality, a reality to which our minds are fitted both by nature and by grace. We make use of words and senses in sacramental life only so as to further this fit.

When we direct our focus through the words and their senses to the reality they mediate, we can trust that God will meet us there. Our minds are made to work the problem to its solution, to get to the bottom of things. Well, no surprise here: God is the solution. Our minds *want* to tend in His direction. The liturgy that God has designed for us through His Church puts "wind into our sails", so to speak, allowing the mind to do what it was made for. We do not have to imagine that paying attention to God is something more mystical than it is. It need not involve feelings, heroic feats of strength, or extraordinary phenomena. It just means holding God in mind and heart, with a peaceful but firm resolution.

In the end, much of our success in this endeavor comes down to *getting out of the way*. The genius of our sacramental life, with its words, senses, and God, is that it gets us out of the way. The sacramental life removes the obstacles to divine grace and facilitates a simple attention to God, aligning our lives more perfectly with their source and end. You may desire to live a holy, contemplative life, and yet continually fall short. Your ambitions and your limitations may be in constant battle. In these circumstances, you can take solace in the uncomplicated power of the sacraments themselves. The best way to grow in holiness is simply to partake in the sacramental life and let God work.

Remember, while here on earth, our aim is to empty ourselves of self-styled identity so that we can welcome the identity of Christ. "You are Christ's; and Christ is God's" (1 Cor 3:23). By setting the right intention and making frequent acts of attention, we offer to the Lord a humble openness, through which Christ can bring about the transformation we so desperately desire.

How then are we supposed to channel our efforts in the sacred liturgy? What should we have in mind and heart? We all know that we need to pay better attention at Mass. We have heard plenty of exhortations to pay better attention. Yet here we are, still limping along. If we are going to make real progress, we need help identifying *how* to pay attention.

Think of a parallel example. Say you are hiking in a beautiful region with your friend. The whole day long, your friend is marveling at landscape after landscape, pleading with you to share in his experience. For whatever reason, though, you do not see it like he does. All you see is one rock formation after another. Sure, it is interesting, but it is not as glorious to you as it is to your friend. But then at the end of the day, something changes. As the sun sets and twilight approaches, the mountains take on new hues. What had seemed like an overexposed stock computer background is now aflame with reds, oranges, blues, and purples. At the magic hour, you finally see the mountains as they are meant to be seen. A new light has shown you how to appreciate the scenery you have been traversing for hours.

In what follows, we want to show the sacrament of the Eucharist in its proper light, to see the liturgy as Christ intends it to be seen. We want to see how Christ is already at work in the signs of the Mass, drawing our attention to Himself and aligning our gaze with his. If we can make small strides in this effort, then the words and senses will, in due course, conduct us to the God whom they signal, and what may seem familiar will burst forth in color.

The Most Holy Eucharist employs a threefold signification. It signifies something that is past, something that is present, and something that is future. Each sign brings along with it the reality (or realities) that it signifies. As to the past, the Eucharist signifies the mysteries of the life of Christ. As to the present, it signifies the graces and virtues that it contains. As to the future, it signifies the unity of the mystical body as it will exist in heaven. As Saint Thomas writes in the *Office of Corpus Christi*: "How holy this feast in which Christ is our food; his passion is recalled; grace fills our hearts; and we receive a pledge of the glory to come" (*Magnificat Antiphon*).[4] In signifying these things, the holy Mass brings them all to bear in the life of the believer. It does what it says it will. In the remainder of this chapter, I will introduce these three signs in a summary fashion before treating them each at length in the following chapters.

## Making Present Past Mysteries

Let's think first about the past. More specifically, let's think about the mysteries of the life of Christ. Our Lord's deeds and sufferings in the flesh are shot through with the fullness of divine life. Each of His mysteries, then—though situated in the historical past—remains mystically available for our commemoration and application through the celebration of the sacraments. The sacred liturgy reaches back into the past and lays hold of these mysteries so that we might profit from them here and now.

As we know, Christ's life in the flesh overflows with grace. From His conception to His Ascension, all that He does and suffers brims with infinite love and infinite merit. Nevertheless, certain parts of His life—and one part in particular—communicates this love most powerfully. This

[4] Thomas Aquinas, Magnificat Antiphon, Vespers for the Solemnity of Corpus Christi, in The Liturgy of the Hours, vol. 3, trans. ICEL (New York: Catholic Book Publishing, 1975), 622.

part is, of course, the Paschal Mystery. In our Lord's Passion and death, we behold just how much God loves us—and just how precious we are to Him. "It is before the abyss of Jesus' agony that we begin to fathom God's love for us."[5]

The Passion represents the culmination of Christ's life in the flesh, for He intends that the whole of His life proceed *toward* the Passion. "The entire life of Christ", itself lived as an expression of the Father's love, "glows by anticipation with the fires of His Passion."[6] The Paschal Mystery, thus, offers the most compact and potent statement of God's saving purpose. "For God so loved the world that he gave his only-begotten Son, that whoever believes in him should not perish but have eternal life" (Jn 3:16).

It is no surprise, then, that in the celebration of the Most Holy Eucharist, which is the "sacrament of love", Christ's Passion and death are especially present. The Mass presents these mysteries in a peculiar fashion, commemorating and applying them in a way that makes it easy for us to recognize them and receive them. As Saint Augustine once preached, "[W]hile he [God] made you without you, he doesn't justify you without you."[7] Through the sacraments, God addresses Himself to our human understanding and choice. The salvation that Christ accomplished on Calvary will not be effected "in some mechanistic way, without one's own willing or participation; rather, the believer is invited to accept in faith the gift that is being offered and to receive the supernatural life that is given to those who participate in this mystery."[8] The Eucharist

[5] Charles Journet, *The Mass: The Presence of the Sacrifice of the Cross*, trans. Victor Szczurek (South Bend, IN: St. Augustine's Press, 2008), 13.

[6] Ibid., 15.

[7] Augustine of Hippo, Sermon 169.13, in *Sermons* III/5 *(148–183) on the New Testament*, trans. Edmund Hill, O.P. (New Rochelle, N.Y.: New City, 1992).

[8] Lawrence Feingold, *The Eucharist: Mystery of Presence, Sacrifice, and Communion* (Steubenville: Emmaus Academic, 2018), 112, n. 101.

provides the means to this participation, to this exercise of our freedom. It is our chance to "believe" in the Son who has been lifted up on the Cross, and so to receive eternal life (see Jn 3:16).

Let's dig into this a bit more. How exactly does the Mass "signify" the saving Passion of Christ? We can look to the twofold consecration. In the celebration of the Mass, the priest consecrates the bread (become the body of Christ) and the wine (become the blood of Christ) in separate ritual acts. We refer to this as *exsanguination*, that is, the blood comes out. The separating of His blood from His body in the Holy Mass refers us sacramentally to the draining of His blood from His body on Calvary. This sign of exsanguination makes His sacrificial death sacramentally present along with the graces of that death.

Christ Himself forges this connection between the Passion and the Eucharistic liturgy at the Last Supper. On Holy Thursday, He is present to His Apostles in the flesh. Though He will not die until the following day, He makes His *Passion* sacramentally present by anticipation. In doing so, He also makes *Himself* sacramentally present in His body and blood. "Now as they were eating, Jesus took bread, and blessed, and broke it, and gave it to the disciples and said, 'Take, eat; this is my body.' And he took a chalice, and when he had given thanks he gave it to them, saying, 'Drink of it, all of you; for this is my blood of the covenant, which is poured out for many for the forgiveness of sins'" (Mt 26:26–28). The presence of the sacrifice brings with it the presence of the body and blood. From the moment of its institution, Christ wills that a validly celebrated Mass—in making His sacrifice sacramentally present—should make His body and blood sacramentally present.

We should pause to consider just how awesome this sacramental gesture really is. When our Lord Jesus Christ suffered and died on the Cross, He let His blood be *drained* from His body. One drop would have been sufficient for our salvation, but He chose to shed *every drop* for love of us. The Lord laid His heart open, holding nothing back. Speaking of His pierced side, our Lord revealed to Saint Catherine of Siena the depths of this love: "My longing for humankind was infinite, but the actual deed of bearing pain and torment was finite and could never show all the love I had. This is why I wanted you to see my inmost heart, so that you would see that I loved you more than finite suffering could show."[9] We do not need to be very imaginative to conceive how much the Lord loves us. We do not need to grub in the dirt beneath the Cross to uncover a drop of His saving blood, for we have been bathed in its tide. As Saint Catherine teaches us, the Lord went to His Passion as a willing victim. His crucifixion was not a necessary or inescapable punishment imposed from without. He chose this death as the most perfect, most compelling evidence of His love. The extravagance of the gesture is part of its logic. God goes to great lengths to give us a chance to return from our alienation. In the Consecration of His body and blood, we behold the exuberance of this love, which the Lord invites us to recognize and receive.

## Heavenly Food

The Lord is not satisfied with just this one appeal, however. We have seen how the Eucharist makes Christ's life and death mystically present. But, as we know, commemoration is for application, and application requires that the graces of *His* life become the graces of *our* lives. It is precisely these

[9] Catherine of Siena, *The Dialogue*, trans. Suzanne Noffke, O.P. (New York: Paulist Press, 1980), 138.

graces that equip us for our particular identity within the life of the Church. They make us who we are called to be. Above all, they fill us with the love of the Lord, with His very charity. The Eucharist speaks not only of the past, then, but also of the present.

What sign does the Lord use to signify this spiritual upbuilding, this edifying in grace and virtue in the present? In an eminently practical fashion, He uses the straightforward sign of bodily upbuilding. He uses food and drink. Christ appoints the sign of bread to communicate His body. In addressing our deepest hunger for divine love, He offers us solid food. The sign is suited perfectly to the charity it mediates. Bread is a staple food among many peoples and cultures. Whether it is fresh and flaky or hard and hearty, it is often found on the table. Bread sustains. It nourishes. Thus, it proves the perfect sign to communicate the substance of Christian perfection.

Christ appoints the sign of wine to communicate His Blood. In refreshing and delighting our spirits, He offers us a heady drink. Again, the sign is suited perfectly to the charity it mediates. Wine is a staple of festivity, enlivening conversation and facilitating communion. It relaxes the anxious, bolsters the weak, and adds a spark to the otherwise dull. It captures the sober intoxication, the shameless freedom of the Christian borne on by love.

Our Lord does not employ the merely functional or the sickeningly sweet. Rather, He prepares a meal the angels themselves would wish to consume. Saint Maximilian Kolbe was in the habit of saying, "If angels could be jealous of men, they would be so for one reason: Holy Communion."[10] In His body and blood, the Lord gives us

[10]Jerzy M. Domanski, O.F.M. Conv., *For the Life of the World: St. Maximilian and the Eucharist* (New Bedford, ME: Academy of the Immaculate, 1993), 129.

supernatural sustenance and spiritual delight beyond what eye has seen or ear has heard. It comes as no surprise that we thrill at the thought of food and drink; for the same God who permitted us an earthly hunger and thirst holds the key to their heavenly satisfaction.

With each reception of Holy Communion, Christ bestows on us a fuller portion of His divine life, given out in morsels and shared in sips, so that His joy may be in us and our joy may be complete. In the Eucharist, He gives us a foretaste of the heavenly banquet as we prepare at present to partake of God forever.

## One Loaf, One Chalice, One Union

The image of the heavenly banquet brings us to our third and final sign. In addition to past and present realities, the Eucharist also puts us in touch with future realities. We can direct our gaze, then, to the very life of heaven, at which our entire sacramental life aims. In order to appreciate the subtle signification, we will have to look closely at the ingredients of the Eucharistic offering.

When our Lord "fixes his menu" at the Last Supper, He chooses bread and wine. But before they appeared on the table, the elements had to be prepared. As Saint Augustine meditates upon this preparation, he writes, "Our Lord Jesus Christ presented us with his body and blood in those things which are made one out of many. Thus one bread is brought together as one from many grains, the other flows together from many grapes."[11] The matter of the Eucharist reveals to us the reality it conceals. Many grains

[11] Augustine of Hippo, Homily 26.17, in *Homilies on the Gospel of John 1–40* I/12, trans. Edmund Hill, O.P. (Hyde Park, N.Y.: New City Press, 2009).

make up one loaf. Many grapes fill one chalice. Do you see where this is going? In receiving Holy Communion, many Christians *become one Christ*. As the matter is made, so too are the recipients redeemed.

By paying attention to the preparation of the bread and the wine, we enter into the logic of the Eucharistic mystery. As a sacrament—that is, as a sign—our Lord's body and blood bring about the union of the Church. By kindling in us the grace of charity through worthy reception of Holy Communion, Christ draws us together in the Spirit and makes us more perfect members of His mystical body.

This is a strange kind of eating. In the ordinary course of events, when we eat something, it becomes part of us. You eat a piece of bread, and it becomes an energy burst or gets broken down and incorporated into a skin cell. In the extraordinary case that is Eucharistic eating, we eat the body of Christ and become *it*. We become Him. Only in this transformation is the intention of the sacrament fully accomplished.

This unity of the mystical body—or ecclesial union—is the final fruit of the sacrament, the very reason for which it was instituted. "Because there is one bread, we who are many are one body, for we all partake of the one bread" (1 Cor 10:17). As we attend to the preparation, we become one in Him who has "prepared a great banquet, mixed the wines, and set the table" (Prov 9:2 [NLT]).

## Forging Ahead

It is worth noting the simplicity and universality of the signs our Lord employs. They do not require that you attend the most beautiful church in the diocese, that you have a charismatic pastor, or that you possess a theology degree. It is within reach, for each one of us, to attend to these signs and to make use of them in order to progress along the way of our Eucharistic pilgrimage.

On the one hand, of course, it is comforting to know that the way is well-marked. We need never wander for lack of signage. But, on the other hand, it is overwhelming to realize all that we have not noticed up to this point. The Lord is inviting us, through every little detail of the liturgy, to a more heedful attention and a more radical abandonment—and we, meanwhile, are thinking about what is for brunch. That can feel dispiriting at times.

A word of encouragement: Fear not. The Lord does not demand perfect attention at present. He understands your fatigue and distraction, your weariness and your worries. He is not scandalized by your limitations. He created you with them. He redeemed you in the midst of them. Rather than fear, simply turn to Him as He gently draws your attention to Himself with each liturgy. Your pilgrimage route will have ups and downs, twists and turns, blisters and sprains. You are probably not going to arrive at the end for some time yet, and that is okay, because God gives you the whole of a life. That does not mean that you should tarry or dawdle—but it does mean that you only need to concern yourself with taking the next step.

On any pilgrimage, there are bound to be moments during which you are sad and downcast as you suffer delays, setbacks, and injuries. To see this journey to its end, to mount from strength to strength, the Lord only asks that you be faithful. At times it may feel like you are going through the motions. In a certain sense, that is unavoidable, an experience common to all pilgrims. But, as you put in the miles with the genuine hope of arrival, you will find that the way opens up a capacity for greater receptivity, a greater hunger and thirst for food and drink that truly satisfies. As you present yourself each day to the Lord, you dispose yourself to the graces that He bestows with generosity. By working through your present trials, even if imperfectly, you are effectively training for your future trials. It is for you, then, to keep walking: to intend and attend insofar as you can.

Our Christian life is a pilgrimage of patience and perseverance. But we can walk it with conviction because the Lord has been intentional in planning the pilgrim way for us. He has crafted the signs with care. He has seen to all the details of the journey. The itinerary He sets before us promises the adventure of a lifetime. And, what is more, He plans to walk it with us. As Saint Charles de Foucauld writes:

> You dwell, my Lord Jesus, in the Holy Eucharist. You are here ... in the Tabernacle. Your body, your soul, your humanity, your divinity, your whole being is here in its twofold nature. How close you are, my God, my Savior, my Jesus, my Brother, my Spouse, my Beloved. You were no nearer to the Blessed Virgin and Saint Joseph in the cave of Bethlehem, in the house at Nazareth, than you are to me here now.[12]

If we read the signs and welcome the graces they indicate, we can not only arrive at Christ, but we can also journey with Christ. By aiming our intention and attention "Godward", we can learn to walk with the Lord all along our pilgrim way.

[12] Charles de Foucauld, *Meditations of a Hermit*, trans. Charlotte Balfour (Providence, R.I.: Cluny, 2023), 50.

## Chapter 5

# Offering It Up

Although our project in this book is to investigate our identity, there is clearly a danger in exploring this question. If we are not careful, we can get stuck in an egocentric trap. When we are constantly immersed in conversation with ourselves and about ourselves, who is going to provide a fresh insight or offer a way forward?

What is more, the danger does not go away simply by "including" God in the conversation. We should not content ourselves with simply involving God in a quest for self-discovery, as a pious afterthought. He is more than just the guarantor of our well-being or the divine answer key to our human homework. The truth is that our identities are of secondary importance, because God's identity is of primary importance. He is not here for our self-realization. We are here for His glory.

God is not something for us to use. In fact, He defies use. He is the ultimate purpose of all worthwhile pursuits, and all things were created for Him (see Col 1:16). To treat Him as a means to some other end would be upside-down or backward, utterly out-of-step with the nature of things. Fortunately, God does not permit Himself to be used for our own lesser aims. He resists our little schemes even as He draws us into His great designs.

The liturgy teaches us this truth, for it ushers us into the presence of God with no thought of His usefulness. It subjects us to God, our Creator and Redeemer, for the purpose of *worship*. By attending to the liturgy, and specifically to its signs, we are brought before God to praise Him and adore Him. The objectivity of liturgical actions does not, however, render them "impersonal". Worship has real effects on the worshipper. As we repeat the words and rehearse the gestures, as we place ourselves before the altar week after week and day after day, we suddenly find that our lives have been transfigured. In trying to make sense of God, we are delighted to find that He has made sense of us.

In this chapter, we will highlight a particular aspect of the liturgy and its effect on us—namely, the Eucharist's "past" signification, the Passion of our Lord Jesus Christ. In the last chapter, we saw how the twofold consecration of the bread and the wine signifies our Lord's sacrifice on Calvary in which He poured out His blood for love of us. Here, we focus especially on the logic of sacrifice. The Mass brings Calvary to bear in the here and now. In effect, the sacrifice of the Mass mystically represents or commemorates the sacrifice of Calvary. It is not a new sacrifice. It is a *new presence* of Christ's one saving sacrifice. The Mass applies or dispenses the merits of this sacrifice, making its graces available to us throughout the course of our lives, touching us daily with the power of His Passion.

Christ's sacrifice is the most perfect expression of worship, and through the Mass, Christ offers us a genuine share in it. We can imitate *His* worship. We can offer *His* sacrifice. And in turning to God as our end in the spirit of Christ's worship, we will receive—as if by surprise—our own identity, too.

## We Are Not Our Own

In coming before God, we recognize at some level that we are not our own. We have our lives on loan from Him, as a gift from Him. In moments of clarity, the desire arises spontaneously to acknowledge our dependence and to respond to God in a spirit of thankful justice. We want to give God what we owe Him, to render it back to Him as praise.

We are all familiar with the claims of human justice. We owe our parents respect and gratitude. We owe our bosses deference and obedience. We owe our friends availability and generosity. In our relationship with God, however, the debt is both more substantial and more foundational. We do not just owe Him this thing or that thing. We owe Him *everything*.

God is the point of our lives. He is their source and their end. Over the course of our lives, we can choose to acknowledge this fact or not. The choice to confess His sovereignty is what we mean by "worship". Admittedly, God does not need our worship, just as He does not need our prayers. Worship is itself His gift. It is how He draws us into His divine life, so that we know and delight in Him as He knows and delights in Himself for all eternity.

God blesses us with freedom precisely for the sake of worship. We see this clearly in the Exodus story. From the burning bush, God instructs Moses on how to address Pharaoh: "Say to him, 'The Lord, the God of the Hebrews, has met with us; and now, we beg you, let us go a three days' journey into the wilderness, *that we may sacrifice to the Lord our God*'" (Ex 3:18; emphasis added). Moses does not lead Israel forth from Egypt just to improve their quality of life or to distance them from their pagan overlords. He leads Israel forth for the sake of *worship*.

Each of us is called, therefore, to praise God for the many gifts He has bestowed on us. We can never worship God sufficiently, as if to say, "Well, glad that is done!" There is always more to know in God and thus always more to love and adore. As Ben Sira writes, "When you praise the Lord, exalt him as much as you can; for he will surpass even that. When you exalt him, put forth all your strength, and do not grow weary, for you cannot praise him enough" (Sir 43:30). Worship is a life's calling, a sweet yoke to bear throughout the whole length of our days.

By embracing our dependence upon God and directing our praise to Him, we are reconciled to God and abandoned more wholly to His divine plan. Worship makes us better creatures and disposes us to the sweet and strong indications of the divine plan in our lives. Worship conducts us along life's way, making us more ourselves, readying us and mobilizing us for our real lives.

## An Offering of Soul and Body

How, then, do we shape a life of worship? And what are the concrete ways in which we can embrace our dependence and direct our praise?

Worship comes in a variety of forms, both interior and exterior. We call the interior offering of the heart "devotion". The devout worshipper wants to give God something of lasting worth and to do so promptly and zealously. He looks around only to discover that everything is already *from* God. And so, with a mix of resignation and resolution, he offers God *himself*. As the English poet Christina Rossetti has it, "What can I give Him, poor as I am? If I were a shepherd, I would bring a lamb; If I were a Wise

Man, I would do my part,—Yet what I can I give Him, Give my heart."[1]

If devotion is the heart of worship, then prayer is its mind. Saint John Damascene describes prayer as "the ascent of the mind to God or the petitioning of God for what is fitting".[2] Together with devotion, prayer strains toward God from the heights of our personality. Prayer offers our worshipful insight to God, alternately expressed in acts of adoration, contrition, thanksgiving, and supplication.

Religious worship also gives rise to bodily movements. Think here of signs of the cross, genuflections, prostrations, and other gestures. Saint Dominic, with his nine ways of prayer and devotion to the most holy Rosary, was especially well-known for his Incarnational approach to the Christian life. This bodily dimension of religion helps us to "flesh out" the spiritual dimensions of devotion and prayer. As human beings, we are embodied souls (or ensouled bodies). We are neither angels without a bodily life nor brute animals without a spiritual life. We live at the horizon of creation, where the bodily and spiritual meet. Our worship reflects this complexity, as soul and body work together.

To illustrate the place of both soul and body in worship, let's take a page from Saint Thomas Aquinas. The Angelic Doctor asks why we offer vocal prayer when mental prayer is just as good (or even better). To paraphrase: Why move our lips when we could just move our minds? Saint Thomas gives three reasons. First, when we vocalize prayer, it actually stirs up devotion. The words we speak have a way of moving us interiorly. When we are feeling

[1] Christina Rossetti, "A Christmas Carol", in *Selected Poems by Christina Rossetti* (Hertfordshire, U.K.: Wordsworth Poetry Library, 2001), 161–62.

[2] John of Damascus, *On the Orthodox Faith: Vol. 3 of the Fount of Knowledge* (Yonkers, N.Y.: St. Vladimir's Seminary Press, 2022), chap. 68.

dry, sad, or distracted, reciting a favorite Scripture verse or singing a praise-and-worship song can help us turn our minds and hearts to God. Second, vocal prayer serves as a release valve, letting mental prayer spill into speech. Think of Christ in the Garden of Gethsemane: "He fell on his face and prayed, 'My Father, if it be possible, let this chalice pass from me; nevertheless, not as I will, but as you will'" (Mt 26:39). It can be helpful to diffuse some of the pressure of our interior life through spoken praise or petition. And third, God gave you a voice. It is your responsibility to give it back.

Saint Thomas shows us how to hold the interior and the exterior together in the life of worship. The exterior is for the sake of the interior, and the interior is for the sake of God. Worship, then, is not a burdensome duty but rather a blessed opportunity to reconcile ourselves—soul and body—to the Giver of life. God wants each of us, whole and entire, soul and body. With interior and exterior worship in close association, we set out toward God with all that He has given us.

## The Worship of Sacrifice

In the tradition, Christians have used two different words to describe worship: *latria* and *dulia*. *Latria* is the worship rendered to God alone. It is "what we give God, and only God, because he is God".[3] *Latria* recognizes God as our Creator and End. As an example of *latria*, think of adoration. We do not adore anyone but God, albeit sometimes with the help of images that conduct us to Him (like the Holy Cross).

[3] David Fagerberg, *Liturgical Mysticism* (Steubenville: Emmaus Academic, 2019), 8.

*Dulia* is the "worship" or homage rendered to distinguished angels and men. *Dulia* recognizes another for some created excellence worthy of honor, respect, or esteem. *Dulia* retains a connection to God, of course. As an example of *dulia*, think of veneration—for "God is wonderful in his saints" (Ps 67:36 [DRA]).

These two forms of worship differ in kind and not just degree. This difference is reflected in the way the Church prays. When we say a litany, for instance, we ask the Father, Son, and Holy Spirit to *have mercy on us*. Later in a litany, we ask the saints to *pray for us*. There are certain kinds of prayers we only make to God. There are other kinds of prayers we make to angels and men.

It is at this point that sacrifice enters the conversation. Sacrifice is an act of *latria*, an expression of the highest worship that is directed to God alone. Sacrifice offers to God our perfect subjection and utmost reverence for His surpassing excellence. Sacrifice (*sacrificium*) comes from *sacer*, which means "holy", and *facere*, which means "to make". The primitive meaning of "holy" is simply "set apart" or "set aside" for worship. In effect, sacrifice sets something apart for worship so that God can bless us through that thing. By offering sacrifice, we seek union with God and a share in His favor.

Each ancient culture had its own ways of offering sacrifice. In general, sacrifice meant taking something out of profane use and assigning it to God's use. In the Old Testament, we see grain offerings, peace offerings, sin offerings, and other offerings besides. But the highest and most perfect of these different offerings is the whole burnt offering, called a "holocaust" offering.

The holocaust offering was special because it was *total*. In other offerings, part of the victim was burned on the altar, while the rest of the victim was given to the priest and to the offerer himself to be eaten later. In a holocaust, the animal victim was killed, its blood drained and sprinkled on the altar, and the whole of the host burned to the honor of God. In this solemn offering, one declares God worthy of the *whole*. The logic of sacrifice is taken to its highest realization.

## A Bloody Business

As products of modernity, we struggle with this language. Sacrifice is neither safe nor tidy. In his novel *Till We Have Faces*, C. S. Lewis captures the atmosphere of sacrifice in his description of a fictional cult to the god Ungit. The protagonist describes a dread that comes over her whenever she is in the company of the priest of Ungit. She recounts: "I think that what frightened me (in those early days) was the holiness of the smell that hung about him—a temple-smell of blood (mostly pigeons' blood, but he had sacrificed men, too) and burnt fat and singed hair and wine and stale incense. It is the Ungit smell."[4]

We find this description horrifying, and naturally so. (There is nothing holy about human sacrifice.) Still, it captures a truth we would sometimes rather forget. Sacrifice is an awful thing—a bloody business. It does not tolerate half-measures. Sacrifice is about giving God our whole selves, because He has a right to our whole selves. God is worthy of the choicest offering.

Sacrifice is not about satisfying our subjective needs or making a modest and civilized gift. Sacrifice is meant to proclaim in a dramatic way that we are God's and not our

[4] C. S. Lewis, *Till We Have Faces: A Myth Retold* (New York: HarperOne, 2017), 12.

own. As David Fagerberg stresses, "When we come before God in liturgy, we come to serve him, we are bound to him, enthralled.... If we do not, then it is not God we are worshipping. In liturgy, we are God's slave, he is not ours."[5] The language of slavery is strong, but it gets at what we are trying to communicate. God is worthy of all worship. God is worthy of the sacrifice of our whole selves.

When confronted by this bloody business, we may be tempted to self-preservation. Why offer my life to God when I could just cling to it in its current form? We may suspect that our preoccupation with managing anxiety and avoiding hardship is inadequate. But that does not make the idea of going all-in any less terrifying. What if God changes my life? What if He asks something difficult from me? We can save ourselves the guesswork: God will change us. It will be difficult. But *life* lies in store. "Whoever would save his life will lose it" (Mt 16:25).

All of us are *made for* sacrifice. If we are truly to live, to become our true selves, we must become a total offering to God. If we guard our lives jealously, in a spirit of self-preservation, we will never come into possession of life. We will remain alone. "Truly, truly, I say to you, unless a grain of wheat falls into the earth and dies, it remains alone; but if it dies, it bears much fruit" (Jn 12:24).

## Recovered and Offered Up

The invitation to sacrifice, then, represents an invitation to communion and fruitfulness. By making a sacrifice of our lives, we entrust them to God so that He can make of them what *He* wills. And what He wills is far beyond what we

[5] Fagerberg, *Liturgical Mysticism*, 11.

can imagine or conceive (see Eph 3:20–21). The prospect is terrifying. But it is possible, because Christ has *made* it possible. Christ goes before us. He has already offered the perfect sacrifice in our very flesh. He has reached into our existential loneliness and pulled us out of ourselves. "And whoever loses his life for my sake will find it" (Mt 16:25). By offering Himself, Christ empowers us to offer ourselves in turn.

How exactly does this work? We have said that in the Holy Mass, we *share* in Christ's sacrifice. Is it not enough simply to receive the fruit of His offering in Holy Communion? Do we really need to "join in"? Did He not die so as to *spare* us the hassle?

Certainly, the Lord's sacrifice is more than sufficient to atone for our sins and those of the whole world. In the Paschal Mystery, Christ does for us what we cannot do for ourselves, acting as the unique and universal mediator of salvation. "Christ ... died for sins once for all, the righteous for the unrighteous, that he might bring us to God" (1 Pet 3:18). Our offerings do not improve upon His offering. There is simply no improvement to be had. Still, we need to be careful in how we understand this sufficiency. Christ's offering is not an act of substitution. Rather, it is an invitation to participation. "He did not become man simply to take our place, but to raise us up and to make us one with Him. And if we are to become one with Him, we have to join Him in the offering of His supreme sacrifice and in the perfect worship of God that this entails."[6]

God wants to involve us in the unfolding of salvation, to make us protagonists in His saving work. Why? Because in doing so, we mature to the full stature of blessed life, and, in turn, we become *more like Him*. If a father were to see

[6] Lawrence Feingold, *The Eucharist: Mystery of Presence, Sacrifice, and Communion* (Steubenville: Emmaus Academic, 2018), 390.

his son struggling to tie his shoes, for instance, he could do one of two things. Either, he could bustle over, tie the shoes himself, and move on. Or, he could rehearse the steps with his son and help him to perform the task. We can appreciate how the latter is actually more loving and dignifying. In the life of worship, the Lord engenders our participation. He matures us as worshippers. He makes us like Himself.

This invitation and transformation come through clearly in the Sacred Scriptures. Let's return to Luke 15 where we found the parable of the prodigal son. We often forget that this parable is one of three parables told in quick succession. Each parable speaks of something lost and found.

In the parable of the lost sheep, the shepherd leaves the flock of ninety-nine, recovers the one, and returns home. He then invites his friends to celebrate with him. His relief is understandable, but the invitation is slightly strange. Before he recovered the sheep, he was (presumably) worried about the financial loss. Now, he is hosting a party, spending money and resources on his guests. Who knows, he might have even served them lamb?

The parable of the lost coin tells a similar story. A woman loses one of her ten coins. She lights a lamp, sweeps the house, and finds it. Again, she calls her friends together to celebrate. The text does not elaborate, but perhaps she, too, hosts a party. Again, this means money and resources spent. Who knows, perhaps she ended up "losing" her coin after all!

The first and the second parable help us to understand the third. As we see, the recovered sheep and the recovered coin are not locked away or jealously guarded. In my imaginative interpretation, they are offered up—they are sacrificed. Turn, then, to the third parable. When the father welcomes his son back home, he does not protect the young man from every future anxiety and hardship. The prodigal son is not going to be shielded from responsibility. He will not be spared the difficulties of life. Rather, he is to be reestablished in his identity as a son and then encouraged in his vocation. When he goes forth the next time, it will be with an unshakeable knowledge of who he is and what he is for. In effect, he will be *offered up*. His life is restored to him so that he can give it up.

The same fate awaits each of us. We are meant for life, and life can only be had as the fruit of sacrifice. The thought of being offered up may seem scary. At times we would almost prefer to be jealously guarded, to be excused from life's trials. But lest we be paralyzed at the prospect of what lies in store, Christ Himself is offered up. He exhorts and encourages us along the way.

## The Mass, Our Share in Calvary

So, how can we best respond to Christ's invitation? Is it a mere matter of imagination or personal effort? Have we been missing out on some secret all these years? The Christian tradition responds simply: Look to the Mass.

The sacrifice of the Mass gives us access to the sacrifice of Calvary because it just *is* the sacrifice of Calvary. Saint Augustine explains the basis for this identification in the following way. In each sacrifice, there is a priest, a victim, the God to whom the sacrifice is offered, and a people for whom it is offered. On Calvary, Christ is both priest and victim. He offers Himself to God the Father on behalf of mankind, with whom He shares a human nature. Similarly, in the Holy Sacrifice of the Mass, Christ is both priest and victim. Here, He offers Himself through the instrumentality of the priest to God the Father on behalf of mankind, whom the Mass benefits. The same logic is at work both on Calvary and in the Holy Mass.

The Mass thus enables us to touch the sacrifice of Christ and to profit from the graces set before us on the altar. No human effort is sufficient to grant access to God. The Mass puts us in contact with a worship beyond us, one that transcends our limits, healing and growing us beyond human frailty. By uniting ourselves to the sacrifice of the Mass, we have the assurance that our worship is full and pleasing, because it is *Christ's worship*. Our task is simply to commemorate it and apply it.

Let's break down what we mean by "commemorate" and "apply". Commemoration may sound somewhat technical, but it simply means the re-presentation of a past event and its graces. As we have seen, the sacramental signs of the Mass established in the liturgical rite are the way Christ makes His life in the flesh contemporary to ours. In the twofold consecration of the bread and wine—the sign of exsanguination—our Lord's Passion is made mystically present. The Mass is not a new sacrifice, not a sacrifice other than that of Calvary. It is "totally subordinated and in complete reference to the sacrifice of the Cross".[7] The Mass, we have said, is a *new presence* of the sacrifice of Calvary.

The notion of *application* follows. We say that the Mass applies or dispenses the graces of the Passion. On the Cross, our Lord performed an act of infinite love in obedience to the Father, thereby meriting the reward of our salvation. Yet the full effect of salvation was not to be realized at the time of His Passion, since many generations of human beings had not yet been born. Christ therefore instituted the Mass to dispense the graces of His Passion throughout time and space. In churches and chapels the world over, He continues to distribute His merits, offering His grace in every age. "As often as the memorial of this Victim is

[7] Charles Journet, *The Mass: The Presence of the Sacrifice of the Cross*, trans. Victor Szczurek, O.Praem. (South Bend, IN: St. Augustine's Press, 2008), 34.

celebrated, the work of our redemption is wrought" (Secret for the Ninth Sunday of Pentecost or Prayer over the Offerings for the Mass of the Lord's Supper and the Second Sunday of Ordinary Time). It is through the celebration of the Eucharist that Christ "come[s] into complete possession of the souls of men".[8]

The Mass accompanies us through the whole of our Christian lives. It holds open to us the wounded side of Christ that we might partake of His blood. We are never without access to His saving sacrifice. This is a tremendous consolation and one of the most concrete proofs of the Lord's abiding mercy. When overwhelmed by our own misery, we might be tempted to think: "Christ died in the past, and yet I sin in the present. How can I return to his offer of salvation?" As Saint Ambrose writes, "If, as often as blood is poured forth, it is poured for remission of sins, I ought always to receive it, that my sins may always be forgiven me. I, who am always sinning, ought always to have a remedy."[9] In instituting the Most Holy Eucharist, the Lord concocts the medicine of immortality and lays it up in the cabinet of the Church. At each Holy Mass, we return for a dose. Each time we receive, we are healed of the sickness of sin and grow in the life of grace.

## Making It Our Own

The primary way in which we can offer our lives to God, then, is through a robust participation in the Most Holy Eucharist. By your Baptism, you are consecrated for fitting

[8] Pius XII, *Mediator Dei* (November 20, 1947), §77.

[9] Ambrose of Milan, *On the Sacraments*, trans. T. Thompson (London: SPCK, 1950), bk. 4, chap. 6.

worship. The liturgical rite, with its words and gestures, "activates" this consecration. Note how the prayers of the Mass unite the offering of the people with that of the priest, who represents Christ. "Pray, brethren, that my sacrifice and yours may be acceptable to God ..." "Therefore, Lord, we pray: graciously accept this oblation of our service, that of your whole family ..." "We, your servants and your holy people, offer to your glorious majesty from the gifts that you have given us, this pure victim, this holy victim, this spotless victim ..."[10]

As the prayers of the Mass call forth a spiritual sacrifice, so the gestures of the Mass enact it bodily. You sign yourself with the cross. You admit your guilt aloud and ask for pardon. You situate yourself in salvation history as the Word of God is proclaimed. You present your gifts as the priest and minister make ready the altar. You kneel in adoration at the Consecration. You receive His Eucharistic body, blood, soul, and divinity into your own body. You are sent forth as a witness to Christ. As the priest and people progress through the Mass, they rehearse in their minds, hearts, and bodies the sacrifice offered by our Lord on Calvary. And as we repeat this ritual action, a more and more perfect sacrifice is called forth from us.

This helps us to understand those prayers of the liturgy that beg God to accept the sacrifice of the altar: "Be pleased to look upon these offerings with a serene and kindly countenance, and to accept them, as once you were pleased to accept the gifts of your servant Abel the just, the sacrifice of Abraham, our father in faith, and the offering of your high priest Melchizedek, a holy sacrifice, a spotless victim." Clearly, the Father is pleased to look upon the

[10] *The Roman Missal*, 3rd ed., trans. ICEL (New Jersey: Catholic Book Publishing, 2011), 382, 490, 493.

offering of His Son. As Josef Jungmann notes, "Christ's sacrifice is not concerned. His sacrifice has already been accepted, and accepted definitively."[11] What is at stake here is something else. As is often the case when our prayers suggest a change in God ("thy kingdom come, thy will be done"), we are in fact asking for a change to take place in us. We need to cultivate the worshipful dispositions for a pleasing offering, more worshipful even than those of Abel, Abraham, and Melchizedek.[12] We are to have the very disposition of Christ!

At Mass, we take Christ's virtues for our own—especially His love and obedience—and so we gain the mind of Christ (see Phil 2:5). So, too, we take His worship as our own—especially His praise of the Father and His petition for salvation. In this offering, we submit with Christ to the Father, abandoning ourselves to Him, uniting ourselves to Christ as both priest and victim. This, then, is the perfect sacrifice: the sacrifice of ourselves. As Saint Peter Chrysologus preaches, "God seeks belief from you, not death. He thirsts for self-dedication, not blood. He is placated by good will, not by slaughter."[13] God does not want some further sacrifice or offering. He only wants you.

That means that when you come to Mass, you should bring *everything* with you. Bring your anxieties and your hardships, your doubts and your fears, your conflicts and your failures. Bring your triumphs and your boasts, your dreams and your aspirations, your plans and your projects. Offer all of it to God; let it be lifted up in the prayers and gestures of the Mass. Make a sacrifice of your real life,

[11] Josef Jungmann, *The Eucharistic Prayer*, trans. Robert L. Batley (Notre Dame, IN: Fides, 1963), 17.

[12] See Feingold, *The Eucharist*, 417–18.

[13] Peter Chrysologus, Sermon 108, in *Selected Sermons*, vol. 1, trans. George E. Ganss, S.J. (Washington, D.C.: Catholic University of America Press, 1953).

your whole life. At the Offertory, place it all on the paten, put it all in the chalice. Unite your offering with that of the priest, with that of Christ Himself. The Lord is not interested in a more put-together version of you. He is not interested in an already-saved you. He is interested in *you*. He wants you to entrust Him with your real life, your whole life. He wants you to make a holocaust offering of your real life, your whole life.

You might think: "Surely, the Lord does not want all of my life? He cannot possibly hope to salvage the mess I have made of everything!" That is precisely what He wants, and the Cross is proof. The Cross is an absolute mess, and that is the point. The Lord comes before us shamed and scourged, crowned and crucified to show the lengths to which He will go to meet you in your misery so that He can pull you out of it and into Him. He wants the sacrifice of your life so that He can unite it to His own and offer it to the Father. The Lord wants to bless you; He wants to save you.

## Death to Identity

As we have seen, sacrifice is a bloody business, and it comes at a cost. When confronted by this cost, we might wish it were otherwise. We might wish that our lives were not so hard, that we were not held to such a high standard, that our vocations were not such a weighty matter. We might wish that we could just rest and relax, that Christian life guaranteed prosperity and comfort. And yet, here we are. The truth is that, however difficult the path to Calvary may be, there really are not any other good options.

Death, after all, is inevitable. We all deserve death. When our first parents sinned, they forfeited the immortality that God bestowed on them at creation. "For the wages of sin is death" (Rom 6:23). When we as a human community wandered from God and His grace, we were left to ourselves and, thus, to an inevitable corruption. There is no getting around it. Not one of us will make it out of here alive.

When confronted by this fact, the pagans simply resign themselves. "Seize the day", they repeat, "trusting not in tomorrow." Though they might seem carefree in their carousing, their revelry is in fact a kind of despair. Nothing awaits them in death save pain and emptiness, and so they play out their mortal coil in the hollow happiness of escapism.

As Christians, we have a way to account for death and a way through it. We are not bound to a fatalistic resignation before the prospect of our demise. Rather, we retain a precious freedom, bought for us by Christ's Passion. We need not flee before our impending doom. Christ goes before us in death and promises to meet us there. He has offered His life, made of His life a gift. Thus, we can offer our lives in Him, can make our lives a gift in Him. Taking care of every detail, Christ even appoints *where* we are to meet Him in His death—namely, at the altar.

As we will see, our Lord's sacrifice is an invitation to union. In offering Himself for us, Christ empowers us to offer ourselves back to Him. He does not spare us the difficulty of life; rather, He sanctifies it. As Louis Bouyer writes, "Christ died for us, not in order to dispense us from dying, but rather to make us capable of dying efficaciously."[14] By uniting our sacrifices to His sacrifice, we partake of His redemptive offering and the life that lies beyond. This gets to the heart of our Eucharistic identity.

[14] Louis Bouyer, *The Paschal Mystery: Meditations on the Last Three Days of Holy Week*, trans. Mary Benoit, R.S.M. (London: George Allen & Unwin, 1951), xiv.

In forgetting ourselves and thinking of God, we come into possession of a life (and a holiness) that surpasses understanding. To attain to this life, we must imitate Christ. We must offer our sacrifice in union with His sacrifice. Only in this way can we hope to have "the mind of Christ" (see 1 Cor 2:16). Bouyer continues:

> [T]he imitation of Christ is the very essence of the Christian life. We must have in us the mind that Christ had; we must be crucified and buried and rise with him.... The whole matter is a mystery signifying that we are to be grafted upon him so that the same life which was in him and which he has come to give us may develop in us as in him and produce in us the same fruits of sanctity and love that it produced in him.[15]

Christ has blazed a trail for us unto the fullness of life. To come into this inheritance, to become whom we are destined to be, we must be conformed to Christ in His Passion, death, and Resurrection. We must mount the Cross in communion with our Eucharistic Lord if we hope to rise gloriously with Him at the end.

And so, we have options in life. On the one hand, we can flee death. We can craft for ourselves a pleasant existence, insulating ourselves from difficulty and sparing ourselves the thought of death. We might enjoy a kind of happiness for a time. Inevitably, though, death will find us. And when it does, it will find us alone and utterly unprepared.

On the other hand, we can embrace death. The prospect may terrify you. Assuming responsibility for our lives, making hard decisions and abiding by them, taking the next steps in our vocations—all of these little deaths can prove exceedingly difficult. And yet, through death we

[15] Ibid., xvi.

enter into life, *His* life. On this *via dolorosa*, we have the assurance of constant companionship, for there is no human experience unknown to Christ. He has plunged into the depths of our humanity and salvaged the whole of it.

Here, then, we hold another key to our Eucharistic identity. If we are to come into possession of God and of ourselves, we must die. If we grasp jealously at our identities thinking only of how God can facilitate our own self-realization, we will have missed the point entirely. God is not to be used. He is to be worshipped. By a life of Eucharistic prayer and devotion, we render our lives back to Him who is our source and end. When this proves too much for us (and it will, almost daily), we need only cling to Christ.

# Chapter 6

# Feeding Our Souls

You have probably heard the adage: "Tell me what you eat and I will tell you what you are." This might seem a little simplistic. After all, we are far more than the content of our stomachs. And yet there is something to the insight. What you eat and how you eat contributes to who you are. Maybe you like modest fare to fuel you for a simple life. Maybe you prefer dainty morsels fit for your sense of refinement.

Whatever your gastronomical preferences, the saying rings truer still when it comes to sacramental eating. When we receive Christ worthily in the Most Holy Eucharist, we become like Him. (In fact, we become Him, but more on that later.) We become the saints whom God intends us to be. The Eucharist, the bread of angels, provides us with all the graces we need to become heaven dwellers and our truest selves. In the end, our identity comes down to diet.

## Signs of Nourishment and Delight

Like every sacrament, the Eucharist brings about changes in the world through signs. In the last chapter, we saw how the Eucharist signifies something of the past—the Lord's Passion. By the twofold consecration—the sign of exsanguination—the Passion is brought to bear in our lives. In this chapter, we will see how the Eucharist signifies something of the present—namely, the graces and virtues it bestows upon us. Under the appearance of bread and wine, His body and blood nourish and delight us, enriching our spiritual lives. "[His] flesh is food indeed, and [His] blood is drink indeed" (Jn 6:55).

The signs correspond beautifully to the reality they communicate. We all need to be fed, both spiritually and physically. We know that we rely on food and drink to build up our physical lives. God, condescending to use images we can understand, intends that we rely on food and drink to build up our spiritual lives as well. This basic analogy makes sense even to those of us with very simple faith. The Eucharist is a matter of spiritual diet. We *need* this spiritual food and drink to thrive in the spiritual life.

To strive for holiness without the Eucharist would be like trying to compete for the Olympics while on a hunger strike. You need calories if you are going to succeed. Remember the swimmer Michael Phelps? When he was in the midst of training for the Olympics, his typical breakfast was three sandwiches of fried eggs with cheese, lettuce, tomato, fried onions and mayonnaise; one omelet; a bowl of grits; three slices of French toast with powdered sugar; and three chocolate chip pancakes. Sounds excessive, but when you have set for yourself a lofty and difficult goal, you need energy.

God has set for us a lofty and difficult goal: the fullness of life with Him in heaven. To reach the goal, we need real strength. "Do you not know that the runners in the stadium all run in the race, but only one wins the prize? Run so as to win" (1 Cor 9:24 [NABRE]). We may as well say, *eat* so as to win!

Now, some foods taste good but do not really sustain. Whether it is a candy or a sugary soda, we each have something that we reach for just to please our taste buds or suppress hunger. But afterward, our stomach turns, our eyelids droop, and we vow not to submit to the same temptation again.

By contrast, sometimes food and drink just sustain and do not really taste good. When we approach consumption like a science experiment, it becomes more effort than joy. Whether it is a protein shake slammed between meetings or a gel pack sucked down in the middle of a marathon, it is no fun to treat gastronomy like economy. There are few things so detestable as an energy bar. Sure, we got the necessary nutrients, but could not it have been less awful?

What we want is food and drink that are both delicious *and* nutritious, not just one or the other. God, in His loving kindness, sets just such a table for us in the sacrifice of the Mass. The Eucharist furnishes us with spiritual sustenance in the life of grace, and it does so under the appearance of food and drink that are, frankly, wonderful. Indeed, "Wisdom has built her house, she has set up her seven pillars. She has slaughtered her beasts, she has mixed her wine, she has also set her table" (Prov 9:1–2).

## Bread and Wine

Let's look at the signs God chooses in detail, starting with bread. For many cultures, bread is *the* food of substance, *the* food of sustenance. Bread may not be the most sustaining food in terms of calories, but it is the staple that practically everyone can afford. It is what we all eat, and it has become a sign of basic nutrition.

When I was younger, my family tried to fast on Wednesdays and Fridays, albeit with limited success. (You would be amazed at what counted as a feast day.) Many a Tuesday, we would go to a local bakery to pick out a few hearty loaves in preparation for the coming trial, having learned early on that we could not sustain our efforts eating low-quality bread. The experience was bound to be difficult, but with good bread, it did not have to be fatal. When the Christian tradition recommends that you give up everything, it recommends that you do not give up bread. There are certain things that we just cannot get by without.

Because bread is so important at so many tables, it has become *the* food around which we congregate. To "break bread" with someone is to share your home, to share your life. It has become a sign of hospitality, a sign of fellowship. Sharing bread means that our lives are bound up together, that we share a common love.

Let's turn now to wine. Wine, like bread, is substance and sustenance. It sustains and nourishes us. Many of us have negative associations with alcohol, and for good reason; this may make us cautious with it or skeptical of its goodness. Notwithstanding the bad effects of overconsumption, wine just was and is what you drink at table in many places. In places where clean water is not readily available, wine is practically all you drink. Like bread, it has become a token of basic nutrition.

Obviously, though, wine goes beyond nutrition. Wine fortifies us for the struggles of life. In the Roman legion, a soldier was issued one skin of wine for a daily ration. You might think that an intoxicating drink is poor fuel for a fighter, likely to make him slow and silly. You might also think that he ought to cut back on days when fighting was imminent. The Romans thought just the opposite. On days when the legion entered into battle, each soldier received *two* skins of wine. The Romans knew that wine gives physical and spiritual strength. Beyond mere calories, wine provides courage.

In addition to courage, wine also brings a sense of communion. Life can be difficult, especially when we find ourselves alone. Along the way, we have to confront obstacles and overcome opposition. In this effort, there is nothing quite like a community to bring us through. Obviously, we do not want to abuse wine or become dependent on it in our social interactions, but it *can* help us to engage with others and reach out when we might not otherwise. It can smooth out social situations, lower inhibitions, and free us up to step forward and step out. (Many couples can thank wine—in part—for their meeting and marrying.)

Wine also brings joy and "gladden[s] the heart" (Sir 40:20). Wine breathes into the soul a savor for the good life. It brings with it an atmosphere of hilarity, of celebration and festivity. Wine gets us out of ourselves and onto the dance floor. For all these reasons and more, Saint Albert the Great argued that wine is simply the *best* drink.

So, when it came time to select signs for the Eucharistic meal, our Lord chose the best food and the best drink. He chose signs of substance and sustenance, of hospitality and fellowship; signs of delight and enjoyment, of hilarity and festivity. He who is the Bread of Life and the True Vine chose bread and wine to mediate His grace and virtue. His choice reveals His intention for what takes place on the spiritual plane. Under the appearance of bread, He offers His body, the best imaginable nourishment. Under the appearance of wine, He offers His blood, giving the greatest imaginable delight.

## The Eucharist Gives Life

So, what graces do bread and wine convey as sacramental signs? What are the spiritual "nutrients" gained? To begin with, the Eucharist effects a spiritual *enlivening*. The sixth chapter of John's Gospel gives us a privileged look into this grace: "For the bread of God is that which comes down from heaven, and gives life to the world" (Jn 6:33).

The Eucharist imbues us with *spiritual life*. It suffuses us with the very life of Christ. In the Incarnation, our Lord's divine life wells up into His human life. In the offer of salvation, His divine life overflows His human life and spills into ours. Christ wants us to partake of this life. "I am the bread of life" (Jn 6:35, 48). In the Eucharist, we feed on the God-man and grace floods our souls. Saint Cyril of Alexandria writes, "Since the life-giving Word of God has taken up residence in the flesh, He has transformed it so that it has his own good attribute, that is, life.... For this reason, the body of Christ gives life to those who participate in it."[1] In the natural course of human life, our souls animate our bodies. In the supernatural course of sacramental life, Christ Himself animates our souls. We are endowed with this life at Baptism and are renewed in it with the sacrament of Penance. The Eucharist nourishes us and delights us by sustaining us with the very flesh of the God-man that we might subsist in Him. "He who eats me will live because of me" (Jn 6:57).

The Eucharist, as Christ's glorified body, introduces us into life everlasting: "This is the bread which comes down from heaven, that a man may eat of it and not die. I am the living bread which came down from heaven; if any one eats of this bread, he will live for ever; and the bread which I shall give for the life of the world is my flesh" (Jn 6:50–51). His flesh is glorious flesh. His blood is glorious

[1] Cyril of Alexandria, *Commentary on John*, vol. 1, trans. David R. Maxwell, Ancient Christian Texts (Downers Grove, IL: InterVarsity Press, 2013), bk. 4.520.

blood. Christ gives us the sacrament that we might partake of life everlasting.

In this spirit, the Fathers of the Church sometimes speak of the Eucharist as a cure for mortality—a medicine of sorts.[2] One ancient Eucharistic prayer asks specifically that the Eucharist heal us from sickness: "And make all those who partake to receive a medicine of life for the healing of every illness, and for the strengthening of every advancement and virtue...."[3] The logic here is plain: The Eucharist enriches in us the life of Christ—the risen one, the deathless one.

Now, to describe the Eucharist in these terms can make Holy Communion sound distasteful, as if we were made to gag down a large pill or swallow a bitter tonic. Certainly, the Eucharist requires our intention and our attention, but it is not unpleasant. Recall that this meal is both nutritious *and* delicious. The Eucharist begets delight, even joy. It is "a dish ... for [our fragility], a cup ... for [our] sadness."[4] The sign of wine conveys this beautifully. Wine, we know, inebriates. At times, we drink wine to help us to forget past sadnesses and set aside past burdens. With the Lord's precious blood, we undergo a similar change (but without the headache afterward). "Eat, O friends, and drink: drink deeply, O lovers!" (Song 5:1). As Saint Cyprian writes, the precious blood begets a sober *intoxication*: "[W]hen the Blood of the Lord and the lifegiving cup have been drunk, the memory of the old man is cast

[2] See Ignatius of Antioch, "Epistle to the Ephesians", in *Early Christian Writings: The Apostolic Fathers*, trans. Maxwell Staniforth (New York: Penguin Books, 1987), 66.

[3] "Anaphora of Serapion of Thmuis", in Paul F. Bradshaw and Maxwell E. Johnson, *Prayers of the Eucharist: Early and Reformed* (Collegeville, MN: Liturgical Press Academic, 1975), 95.

[4] Thomas Aquinas, *Sacra solemnis*: "Dedit fragilibus | corporis ferculum, | dedit et tristibus | sanguinis poculum." (Translation mine.)

aside and there is induced forgetfulness of former worldly conversation, and the sorrowful and sad heart which was formerly pressed down with distressing sins is now relaxed by the joy of the divine mercy."[5]

In our lives of Eucharistic worship, we come to discover that life is not against us; life is for us. We forget too easily that God wants to give us life. God does not want our experience of this world to overwhelm us totally. He wants it to enliven us. That is not to say that life should be like an extended hotel stay or an all-inclusive resort. But neither should it feel like a prison. Life is something more like an athletic training facility. (Perhaps some of you would prefer the prison.) God uses our time on earth to train us up, to make us healthy and strong so that we can flourish in the heavenly city. And the appointed diet for this transformation is His body and blood.

God has created us to share in His divine life through the human life of our Lord Jesus Christ. Without God, we can never become who He intends us to be—partakers of His nature and co-heirs of His kingdom. If we are to share in His life, we must receive Him. As C. S. Lewis writes in *Mere Christianity*: "God designed the human machine to run on Himself. He Himself is the fuel our spirits were designed to burn, or the food our spirits were designed to feed on. There is no other."[6] The Eucharist is appointed for precisely this task. As Saint Augustine recounts, God mingles Himself—an invisible food we cannot otherwise ingest—with the visible flesh of man so that we might receive Him.[7] Without this food, we waste away; without

[5] Cyprian, Letter 63.11, in *Letters (1–81)*, trans. Rose Bernard Donna, C.S.J. (Washington, D.C.: Catholic University of America Press, 1964).

[6] C. S. Lewis, *Mere Christianity* (New York: HarperCollins, 2001), 50.

[7] Augustine of Hippo, *Confessions*, trans. F.J. Sheed (Indianapolis: Hackett, 2006), bk. 7.18.

this food, we remain insubstantial. God wants to make us *real*. We must feed on the real if we aspire to the real. We must take our place at His table.

## The Eucharist Gives Us God's Love

What, then, is the nature of this spiritual life apportioned in the Eucharist? It is the life of *divine love*. "So we know and believe the love God has for us. God is love, and he who abides in love abides in God, and God abides in him" (1 Jn 4:16). The Eucharistic elements capture this content. The bread and wine betoken love. In providing substance and sustenance, in furnishing delight and enjoyment, bread and wine signal the love they bestow. Love, we know, calls us together and sustains us in being. Love lowers defenses and enlivens a community.

Love is what makes life worth living. We experience our lives as good to the degree that they are filled with love and marked by meaningful relationships—with God, with family, and with friends. The longest sociological study on human happiness, the Harvard Study of Adult Development, has found that good relationships are the best overall indicator of well-being. The individuals participating in the study consistently report that life is good inasmuch as it is *shared*.

As we know, relationships have to be nurtured. They have to be cultivated. Friends, Aristotle teaches us, have to live together. Love at a distance is love in peril. If we want to grow our relationships, we have to spend time together, pursuing common conversations and common projects. You might say that we feed on the company of those we love, and we must take time to enjoy them.

God wants to share His love with us. He Himself is a communion of persons—Father, Son, and Holy Spirit.

Each reception of Holy Communion promises to intensify the love of the Blessed Trinity in our souls. As we receive the Lord in His body, blood, soul, and divinity, He brings along His love of the Father from whom He comes forth from all eternity. So, too, He brings with Him His love of the Holy Spirit, who fills His soul with grace and virtue.[8] God wants us to abide in His communion that He might commune with us, that He might make our lives a marvel of love. Christ gives us the Eucharist so that we can consume His love and be consumed by it.

## The Love That Is Charity

When we talk about the love of God at work within us, we refer to it as charity. Charity signifies much more than donations given to the material poor. That is part of the story, but not the whole story. Charity is simply the love of God poured into our hearts, the love of God made fit for a human frame. "God's love has been poured into our hearts through the Holy Spirit who has been given to us" (Rom 5:5). Charity is the greatest of the virtues, those strengths of character that empower us to act well toward God and one another. While each of the virtues contributes to our spiritual vitality, charity stands head and shoulders above the rest. Charity makes us live and love on a higher plane, on God's plane. It equips us with everything we need to perform supernatural deeds for supernatural merits with supernatural rewards.

Charity is what counts most in our relationship with God because it is what makes for real union. Charity puts

[8] See Lawrence Feingold, *The Eucharist: Mystery of Presence, Sacrifice, and Communion* (Steubenville: Emmaus Academic, 2018), 512–14.

us in living contact with God—our ultimate end, our highest good, our greatest friend. In effect, charity is just friendship with God. It establishes a common life with God, introducing us into the communion of Father, Son, and Holy Spirit.

Charity brings us before God so that we can commune with Him. This is an important point, because other virtues simply cannot bring you before God. Temperance and fortitude bring you before your own emotions. Justice and prudence bring you before others and your actions. The theological virtues all bring you before God, but not for the same reasons. When faith and hope bring you before God, they come looking for something. Faith looks for revelation. Hope looks for beatitude. But charity just comes looking for God, period. It does not look over or under, around or beyond Him. It just looks straight at God *and says*, "It is good that you are." Charity sets aside any thoughts of cashing out or moving on to the next thing, fixing us instead in a relationship of perfect sustenance and unimaginable delight. Charity lays hold of God with the understanding that He is enough and more than enough.

In a certain sense, charity is the end of the line. It leaves nothing further to be desired or pursued. It cannot be subjected to any other law, for it is the highest law—the law of love. From its place of preeminence, charity orders the whole life of virtue, situating each of our pursuits in its proper place. It also governs the whole of life, motivating our various duties and responsibilities with the added impetus of the love of God. Finally, it perfects and fulfills the whole of life, drawing our activities into the ambience of the friendship with God. Charity shows us what does and does not matter, where this and that thing fit, and why we undertake any of it in the first place. When you think about introducing a little more discipline into your life, for example, charity sees to it that your efforts are not a mere matter of time-management or organization. It makes your efforts, instead, an expression of love for God and others.

The one who lacks charity is, on the spiritual level, nothing. You might have plenty of other virtues that you have acquired over the years. But if you do not have charity, you are effectively a spiritual zero.

> If I speak in the tongues of men and of angels, but have not love, I am a noisy gong or a clanging cymbal. And if I have prophetic powers, and understand all mysteries and all knowledge, and if I have all faith, so as to remove mountains, but have not love, I am nothing. If I give away all I have, and if I deliver my body to be burned, but have not love, I gain nothing. (1 Cor 13:1–3)

You read that correctly. You can have faith in the Triune God and the Incarnate Lord, you can have hope that God will give you eternal life, you can submit to persecution—but if you do not have charity, your faith and your hope are dead.

Our lives are beautiful and wonderful to the degree that they embody and express this charity. God bestows Himself so that we can behold and embrace Him in love. This unshakeable foundation becomes the basis of all holy endeavors. We are destined for this love. As Saint Thérèse of Lisieux writes, "O Jesus, my Love ... my *vocation*, at last I have found it.... MY VOCATION IS LOVE! Yes, I have found my place in the Church and it is You, O my God, who have given me this place; in the heart of the Church, my Mother, I shall be *Love*."[9] This is not just

[9] Thérèse of Lisieux, *Story of a Soul: The Autobiography of St. Thérèse of Lisieux*, trans. John Clarke, O.C.D., 3rd ed. (Washington, D.C.: ICS Publications, 1996), 194.

Thérèse's niche. It is our vocation and the vocation of every Christian.

## The Eucharist Gives Us Christ's Passionate Love

It is worth pausing here to reinforce the link between our current topic and that of the last chapter. The love that we see on display in the Passion is precisely the same love at work in the Eucharist.

God sent His Son precisely in order to communicate His love to us. Christ's life in the flesh is a splendid gallery of this love. On every wall of the exhibit, we see depictions of God's loving purpose. Each of Christ's deeds and sufferings illustrates the depths of His love for us, drawing us into that same love by its beauty and attraction. The ultimate purpose of the exhibit only comes together, however, at the end—in the suffering, death, and Resurrection of Christ.

The Passion of our Lord Jesus Christ tells forth and pours out the love of God in most excellent fashion. On the Cross, we behold the depths of God's love for us and are prompted, impelled even, to love in return. This is by design. God knew that the offering of Calvary was the best way to get our attention and carry His point. He chose the most rank of injustices, the most brutal of tortures, the most harrowing of deaths in the most public of places and at the most terrible of times. Paradoxically, the crucifixion of Christ begets the salvation of man. Christ chooses an exceedingly painful humiliation precisely so as to transform it into our glorious exaltation. These are the lengths to which He will go to show both the wideness of His mercy and the heights of self-offering to which He calls us.

The Lord wants us to love Him, so He shows us He loves us. A cynic might say that is manipulative, but it is not. God does not want our love because He needs the affirmation or the admiration. He wants it because our response *is* our salvation, and God wants to save us. In His divine madness, He lived a life and suffered a death to reveal to us the abyss of divine love so that we might sound its depths.

As He gave His body for us on the Cross, so Christ gives us His body in the Eucharist. In the Passion, the Lord hands Himself over for us. At the altar, He extends that "handing-over" under sacramental signs. The Lord gives us His Eucharistic body to nourish and delight us with the love of His Passion and death. The Eucharist, then, is the sacrament of Christ's passionate love for us, the sacrament of His crucified charity. Its sole purpose is to bestow Christ's love.

## Setting the Table, Burning the Fuel

If we are to enjoy the banquet, then we have to prepare. How, then, should we set our table and whet our appetite so as best to partake of this bounteous feast?

First, we have to be ready to receive. Concretely, this means that we cannot be in a state of mortal sin if we want to approach the altar. As it is instituted, the Eucharist does not pardon mortal sins. It does not put charity where it was not previously. For this pardon, we have the sacraments of Baptism and Penance. The Eucharist is not intended to *light* the flame of charity, but to *fan* it. It is fuel for the fire, not itself a fire-starter. So, just as you would not come to dinner already full, so you would not partake of Holy Communion when already full of something other than God. To enjoy the feast, you have to present yourself with a "hunger and thirst for righteousness", but sin deadens our Eucharistic appetite.

When we receive in a state of grace, though, the Eucharist moves us to realize a fuller love. The grace of sacramental Communion prompts us to address obstacles and hindrances to the perfect reign of charity and to become more zealous in our use of God's gifts. More specifically, it helps us address past sins and avoid future ones. Though it does not pardon mortal sins, it does fortify us against them. So, too, it consumes venial sins in a blaze of love. Venial sins, we know, are those little stumblings of mediocrity, self-regard, and moral ugliness that we frequently commit. They distract and disperse us. While they cannot snuff out charity, they can draw its attention (and our efforts) away from the radicality of love, sapping us of our full fervor. The Holy Eucharist, by inciting charity within us, forgives venial sins and even remits some of their punishment. The grace of sacramental reception burns up the dross of past venial sins and fortifies us for future struggle.

The life of Eucharistic worship consumes us with love of the Lord, leaving less and less place for sin in our lives. As we become more certain and confident in our relationship with God, we have less to do with all that is not of Him, are less likely to betray the love that has taken hold of our lives. The Eucharist does not take away the possibility of sinning entirely, but, like food, it preserves us from the onset of illness, maintaining our spiritual health. It gives us a share in Christ's vigor. For just as His Passion conquered the devil and all his demons who flee before the power of the Cross, so the Eucharist repels all the assaults of demons. As Saint John Chrysostom says: "Like lions breathing forth fire, thus do we depart from that table, being made terrible to the devil."[10]

[10]John Chrysostom, Homily 46.3, in *Homilies on the Gospel of John*, trans. Charles Marriott, in *Nicene and Post-Nicene Fathers*, 1st ser., vol. 14, ed. Philip Schaff (Buffalo, N.Y.: Christian Literature Publishing, 1889).

The effect of the Eucharist goes way beyond the avoidance of sin, however. It draws us into the very heart of God, itself a furnace of love for us. Christ came to share this heart, to kindle us with its flame. "I came to cast fire upon the earth; and would that it were already kindled!" (Lk 12:49). Holy Communion is His way of setting us ablaze. Saint John Damascene likens the Eucharist to the burning coal swallowed by the prophet:

> Let us approach it with burning desire and with our hands folded in the form of a cross let us receive the body of the Crucified, and applying our eyes and lips and foreheads let us partake of the divine coal, so that the fire of the desire within us might receive the heat of the coal and burn up our sins and illuminate our hearts and so that by partaking of the divine fire we might be set on fire and deified.[11]

By receiving the Most Holy Eucharist, we are drawn into the heart of God and inflamed by His light and heat. In this exchange, we come to glow with the ardor of divine love.

Over the course of a life of sacramental reception, the Eucharist promises to make us free—free to live, free to love, free to revel in God's gift. Each day, at the banquet of His love, He lavishes upon us a Eucharistic delight and liberates us with a spiritual intoxication. As we feed on His body and drink His blood, we come to live with an indomitable joy and a reckless abandon.

## Do You Not Desire Me?

A friend of mine tells the story of a man in his parish who came often to the church but did not receive. For years he

[11] John of Damascus, *On the Orthodox Faith: Vol. 3 of the Fount of Knowledge* (Yonkers, N.Y.: St. Vladimir's Seminary Press, 2022), chap. 86.

attended daily Mass, not once approaching the altar. By his own admission, the man had a divided heart. At the time, he was in a somewhat stable same-sex relationship, and he did not want to break it off. So, he continued to attend Mass, but at a distance of his own choosing. One day, though, everything changed. As the majority of the congregation presented themselves for Holy Communion and he knelt unmoved in his place, he experienced something entirely new. From the host, he heard the Lord ask him a simple question: "Do you not desire me?" With that question, the walls came down. Shortly thereafter, he made the difficult decision to separate from his partner. He sought out the sacrament of Penance and began to receive the Eucharist on a daily basis.

God burns with desire for you, and He asks you the same question: "Do you not desire me?" He wants to live the same life as you, to think the same thoughts as you, to love the same things as you. He wants to inhabit you, to be closer to you than you can even imagine. There is no bound to this love. As proof of His love, God gives you a taste of His infinite desire. He wants you to burn with desire for Him, to hunger and thirst for Him. He will not have you compromise on this desire. To settle for anything less than Him would be hell, and He wants you to live with Him in heaven.

In sharing something of His infinite desire, God has ruined your chances for this-worldly contentment. You will never find any creature that corresponds fully and perfectly to your bottomless need. He has given us an appetite for Himself, and for the time being, we remain as yet unsatisfied. As Saint Catherine of Siena writes of God, "You, eternal Trinity, are a deep sea: The more I enter you, the more I discover, and the more I discover, the more I seek you. You are insatiable, you in whose depth the soul is sated yet remains always hungry for you, thirsty for you, eternal Trinity, longing to see you with the light in your light."[12] But why would God do this? Why would He feed us on His fullness only to leave us unsatisfied? The secret lies in love. By maturing us through a life of Eucharistic worship, God furthers us in the life of charity. In the process, He increases our capacity both for Him and for satisfaction. Over the course of our lives, God promises to provoke a deeper hunger and refine a subtler appetite, so that we become capable of a richer participation in His divine life. It is not just that we are weak and in need of strength or impure and in need of cleansing. So too, we are destined for the heights of blessed life, and our Eucharistic diet creates both the space and the desire for this transformation. Ultimately, there is hope that satisfaction lies in store. If we remain steadfast throughout the course of our lives, the longing that we experience will lead us all the way to the fullness of the heavenly banquet, where God will be all in all.

The journey that lies before us will prove difficult, but God has provided food and drink for the way. His body and blood are our daily ration, a heavenly fare that somehow increases our desire even as it increases our delight. As David Fagerberg writes, "If you taste and see, you will see that you have not tasted enough yet. The sacraments are not designed to fulfill our appetites, they are designed to increase those appetites. The sacraments should not satisfy us, they should increase our thirst."[13]

By fanning love into flame, the Holy Eucharist has us flit heavenward with ever greater ardor. As we feed on His body and blood, He nourishes us with His infinite love

[12] Catherine of Siena, *The Dialogue*, trans. Suzanne Noffke, O.P. (New York: Paulist Press, 1980), 364.

[13] David Fagerberg, *Liturgical Mysticism* (Steubenville: Emmaus Academic, 2019), 115.

even as He consumes us with desire for the realities that lie in store. The Eucharist is but an earthly foretaste of the heavenly feast. The Eucharistic meal is not your thirty-minute unpaid lunch break. It is not about "getting the job done". It is about communing with the Lord with whom you will dwell for eternity. And while it is as hearty as the love it bears, still it signals a fuller fare—the fullest fare—to those who observe the logic of love. In the meantime, the menu is clear enough: Take and eat, take and drink. In due course, you will become what you receive.

# Chapter 7

# Becoming the Body

There is a strange tension at work in our lives. On the one hand, we want to be special, unrepeatable, unlike anyone else. We want a sense of our unique excellence. On the other hand, we want to belong, to fit in, to be included. We want to be part of something bigger than ourselves and to contribute to it.

In recent decades, we have seen this tension play out in the broader culture around the questions of sexual orientation and gender. By identifying with a particular sexual orientation or a particular gender, many people are able to tap into powerful currents of both uniqueness and belonging. Laying claim to a nontraditional sexual orientation or gender imparts a sense of rarity and value. You only need to watch a few minutes of a Pride parade to recognize that, for those involved, this is something of great personal significance. At the same time, the LGBTQ+ movement places a huge emphasis on mutual support and is often very vocal and visible in its expressions of solidarity.

So just as coming out or identifying confers a sense of individuality, so too it yields a sense of community. The momentum this movement has gained should not surprise us. It answers to a particular need of the human heart, and many feel that this need is met when they make their orientation or gender known. They hear, as if for the first time, you are *special* and you are *one of* us. The power of affirmation and acceptance cannot be overstated. In a world where many have suffered and been lonely for so long, why should they ever doubt, much less leave behind, the people who seem to want what is good for them?

This strange tension is present in the questions we bring before our Eucharistic Lord. All of us want both to be unique and to belong. All of us sense that the meaning of our lives is both deeply individual and inherently communal. This goes all the way down to our grammar: the word "I" does not even make sense except in relation to a "you" or a "we". We figure out who we are in and through relationships—with our family, colleagues, and friends. Ideally, these ties help us come to a true affirmation of and appreciation for our identity, but there is no guarantee. It is hard to find your fit in the midst of others who have not found theirs. Estranged siblings, self-centered colleagues, and equally perplexed friends are not always the best help. The mounting pressure to both stand out and fit in leaves us harried and confused, unsure where to turn for answers.

We need a better way. We need an identity in which we can both repose and mature. We need conversations and relationships beyond our earthly resources. We need heavenly help.

This brings us to the final sign we set out to explore: Out of many grains, one loaf; out of many grapes, one chalice; out of many Christians, one body of Christ. By the power at work in this sign of future realities, we are drawn into the union of the mystical body to be realized fully in eternity. In the life of Eucharistic worship, we become more perfectly members of the body of Christ. In the course of this transformation, we discover ourselves as uniquely beloved by God and wholly belonging to our brothers and sisters as the Lord furnishes us with graces and virtues suiting us to our vocation in the Church and the world. Each of us is made to tell forth the glory of God in a singular way, determined by God's peculiar and particular love for us. But we can only fulfill that call if we are first incorporated into the body of Christ and identified with Him. The Eucharist constitutes us, together with the whole people of God, as the one worshipping Christ. In the unity of His body, we have our place for all eternity, taken up in the joy of glorifying the Father. And as we shall see, that eternity has already begun in the here and now.

## The Most Intimate Union

We said above that the Eucharist reveals the Lord's unique love for *you*. Your life in the Church is ineradicably personal. You are not simply a body in a pew, essentially replaceable by anyone else. As Saint Thérèse reminds us, "Jesus is there in the Tabernacle expressly for *you*, for *you alone*; He is burning with the desire to enter your heart."[1] The Lord unfolds this love in your life with an offer of genuine intimacy. Let's take a closer look.

Love expresses itself in closeness. It does not keep its distance, affirming from afar or bestowing from on high. That would be to accentuate the difference between lover and beloved. Rather, the lover wants to be close, to be "on the same level" as the beloved. God expresses Himself in just such closeness. He does not leave space between Himself and His beloved. Certainly, He condescends, but He

[1] Thérèse of Lisieux, "From Thérèse to Marie Guérin [May 1889]", in *General Correspondence*, vol. 1, *1877–1890*, trans. John Clarke, O.C.D. (Washington, D.C.: ICS Publications, 1982), 568.

does not patronize. He draws near, and when He does, He ennobles and dignifies His beloved.

God has been close to us from the dawn of creation up until the present moment, sustaining our being and giving us life:

> Where shall I go from your Spirit?
> Or where shall I flee from your presence?
> If I ascend to heaven, you are there!
> If I make my bed in Sheol, you are there!
> If I take the wings of the morning
> and dwell in the uttermost parts of the sea,
> even there your hand shall lead me,
> and your right hand shall hold me. (Ps 139:7–10)

There is simply no escaping God, even if we wanted to. Our Creator is present to each person in every time and place, without exception.

But God wants to crown this closeness by a yet more intimate union. The Incarnation reveals the intensity of His desire. In our Lord Jesus Christ, we see how close God has come to our humanity. It is a kind of promissory note. As it is for the natural Son, so, too—by analogy—will it be for the adopted sons and daughters. God wants to dwell within each of us. "Behold, I stand at the door and knock. If any one hears my voice and opens the door, I will come in to him and eat with him, and he with me" (Rev 3:20). In His incarnate life, and especially in His Passion, Our Lord overcomes whatever distance separates us from Him. And by the life of grace, especially through the sacrament of the Eucharist, He reaches beyond that distance into the innermost depths of our being. From the altar, the God of the universe asks to enter into your heart in order to "eat" with you.

The painting "The Light of the World" by William Holman Hunt portrays with striking clarity the intimacy

God desires. In the painting, Christ is knocking at a door. He is not receiving a warm welcome as He stands alone on an empty street late at night. The door clearly has not been opened in a long time, as weeds have grown up around it. A closer look reveals a strange detail: the door has no handle on the outside. Why, you might ask? Is it simply defective? Presumably, the only handle is *on the inside.*

The allegory is clear enough. The door is the entry to the human heart. This entry is shut up, perhaps signifying stubborn unconversion. There is little coming and going at this door between the inhabitant and his Lord. And yet, a choice remains: Christ beckons. If the Lord is to pass in, He must be admitted willingly. Man must welcome the offer of grace and admit Christ, the Light of the World, into his life.

This image captures a radiant truth, but a slight alteration to the painting can help us perceive a still more radiant truth. Imagine for a moment that Christ is within, and *you* are standing out on the street. As our Creator, Christ is already nearer to us than we are to ourselves. He is present in our innermost being. From this perspective, we can see the situation of the unconverted still more clearly. It is *we* who are locked out, alienated from our true selves. It is we who have to knock at the door of our own hearts so that Christ can let us in. We will not be fully alive or fully ourselves until we do so, for we are meant to abide with Christ in the life of grace. This life renovates and adorns our interior lives by a yet more perfect union.

This gives us an appreciation for what Christ is doing when we receive Holy Communion. As our Creator, He is already at work within us. Nevertheless, He takes our flesh and institutes the Eucharist so as to be more perfectly at work within us, to draw even closer still. What could be closer to us than the food we eat? It is literally incorporated into us! Christ wants to dwell at the center of your being so that you might abide with Him there.

## The Priority of the Body

In emphasizing the intimate and mystical union that Christ seeks with the individual soul, however, we must not lose sight of another essential truth: Partaking in the life of Christ is a communal affair. None of us partakes alone. When we enter into relationship with Christ, we enter into relationship with all of the brethren. What is more, this community has *pride of place* over our individuality. In the life of the Church, the "we" has priority over the "I". The mystical body, constituted by the Eucharist, is more than just an aggregate of individual sanctities. It is the one body of Christ, head and members.

All of this talk of community might be cause for worry. It would be a shame if we sacrificed our special selves just to fit into an un-special assemblage. What of our individuality? How can we be treasured as parts of a whole? Who is to say that we will be known and loved in this mystical (and seemingly amorphous) body? Harboring such suspicions, many of us cling to identities of our own fashioning. We struggle to entrust ourselves to others.

But we can trust the Lord with our lives. He will not pass us over or grind us down. He apportions each of us a place and a role in His mystical body, one that is precious to Him and borne of an intensely personal love. So: we can relax! When we offer up our anguished and unstable individuality, we receive something infinitely better in return—Christ, each other, and ourselves. We just have to be small and play our part.

To take a personal example, I remember being very nervous that I would lose a certain *joie de vivre* when I entered religious life. Monks and friars seemed so serious and stolid to me. I worried that I would have to undergo an artificial change of personality in order to fit in, so I stubbornly resisted my superiors when they tried to temper my exuberance or cool my zeal. As it turns out, all I resisted were their efforts to address my immaturity and insecurity. My so-called *joie de vivre* was in truth mixed up with personality defects that were undermining my religious formation. Once I began to trust my superiors and let go of my faulty sense of self, a deeper joy lay in store.

It is no surprise that many of us fear the prospect of being cogs in a machine, especially given the ways we have seen social and political power abused in recent history. Rather than entrust ourselves to a scary collective, we would rather hold ourselves at a distance and make our Christian life an individual project. Holiness, we say to ourselves, is just Jesus and me, a personal relationship involving no one else.

The hard truth is this: while you might save yourself some hurt with this approach, you will undoubtedly miss out on the deepest joys of the life of grace. By keeping aloof, not only do we remain captive to immaturity and insecurity; we also deprive ourselves of God's infinite riches. If I remain at a distance, then I am cut off from the work He is accomplishing in the Church as a whole. I miss out on my graces; I miss out on the graces given to others; I miss out on the life of the body, its beauty and vitality. Seen from afar, the Blessed Virgin Mary is a cold and intimidating monument of graces I will never enjoy; her exaltation is my humiliation. Seen up close, however, she is my mother and mediator, my advocate and guide; I discover that the superabundant charity that God has poured into her heart is turned toward me, exercised upon me. As I am made more and more a member of the body, her graces become more and more my graces. As a member of the body, I am able to enjoy both the gifts given to me and those that are given to the brethren.

The liturgy is our greatest help in cultivating this higher communion. As Pope Benedict XVI writes, "The goal of eucharistic communion is a total recasting of a person's life, breaking up a man's whole 'I' and creating a new 'We'."[2] In Eucharistic worship, each of us offers himself in union with Christ for the glory of God and the salvation of souls. Through the liturgy, we are all inserted into God's plan and made one in its service. The liturgy is thus a "supraindividual prayer". It is beyond any one of us. It is not subject to the whim of any one person; although it unites each of us to Jesus, it is not our "alone time" with Him. God gives us the liturgy to draw us together in worship and incorporate us in His body.

## Our Place in the Body

The Christian tradition, drawing on Scripture, has a tried-and-true image for thinking about difference without inequality: the image of the body. We are so used to speaking of the "Body of Christ" that it is possible to go a long while without thinking through the metaphor. Saint Paul lays it out in his letter to the Corinthians:

> For just as the body is one and has many members, and all the members of the body, though many, are one body, so it is with Christ.... For the body does not consist of one member but of many. If the foot should say, "Because I am not a hand, I do not belong to the body," that would not make it any less a part of the body. And if the ear should say, "Because I am not an eye, I do not belong to the body,"

[2] Joseph Ratzinger, *Behold the Pierced One: An Approach to Spiritual Christology*, trans. Graham Harrison (San Francisco: Ignatius Press, 1986), 89.

> that would not make it any less a part of the body. If the whole body were an eye, where would be the hearing? If the whole body were an ear, where would be the sense of smell? But as it is, God arranged the organs in the body, each one of them, as he chose.... The eye cannot say to the hand, "I have no need of you," nor again the head to the feet, "I have no need of you." On the contrary, the parts of the body which seem to be weaker are indispensable.... If one member suffers, all suffer together; if one member is honored, all rejoice together. Now you are the body of Christ and individually members of it. (1 Cor 12:12–27)

As with any body, there is genuine differentiation. Incorporation into Christ does not mean we get pureed into a homogenous soup. Rather, we become eyes and ears, knees and elbows, hands and feet. We become organs, distinct from one another and yet unintelligible without reference *to* one another. Our identities are unique but cannot be had in isolation. Our lives are oriented to Christ, their source and end, in union with our brothers and sisters.

God bestows different gifts as testimony to His divine creativity and abundance. Each of us manifests and communicates His divine life in some peculiar and particular way. Yes, God loves each of us with the same unconditional love. But He does not love us all in exactly the same way; He loves us differently, that is, uniquely. That difference is expressed in the unique gifts, talents, and functions we bring to the body.

In some lives, His gifts are especially obvious. We can think of great miracle workers or saints with public apostolates. In other lives, His gifts are less obvious. You can think here of those hidden saints with whom you live and work. But in every case, God gives *enough* and *more than enough*. As Saint Thérèse's sister Pauline once taught her, though we may have different capacities, God intends to fill each of us to the brim: "[And] in heaven God will grant

His Elect as much glory as they can take, the last having nothing to envy in the first."[3]

Concretely speaking, this means that God is doing something good in you. It may not be the most obvious thing, but it is good. The image of the body helps us to understand. The goodness of a hip or a heel lies in being and doing what a hip or a heel is supposed to be and do. Its goodness is relational—to other parts of the body—and purposeful—toward the end of human life. God has not endowed you with gifts so that you can wander off and simply admire them. He has endowed you with gifts to draw you into communion and to achieve the aim for which He made you.

## Doing Away with Comparison

Now the painful questions: Why did He not give me better gifts? Was it an accident? Did He somehow fail in His responsibility? Here, we can draw on Paul's wisdom: "And if the ear should say, 'Because I am not an eye, I do not belong to the body,' that would not make it any less a part of the body" (1 Cor 12:16). In the context of the body, the Apostle suggests, a sorrowful sense of insignificance is just as silly (and dangerous) as an exaggerated sense of self-importance: "I have no need of you" (1 Cor 12:21).

God chose to give you this life (and not another) as the concrete expression of His infinite love for you and for His Church. Let that sink in. You are a delight to the Father and a gift to His Church. He does not will for you the identical graces that He wills for Christ, for Mary, for Saint Joseph, or for anyone else—because He does not love you

[3] Thérèse of Lisieux, *Story of a Soul: The Autobiography of St. Thérèse of Lisieux*, trans. John Clarke, O.C.D., 3rd ed. (Washington, D.C.: ICS Publications, 1996), 45.

in the same exact way He loves Christ, Mary, Saint Joseph, or anyone else.

But why did He arrange it this way and not that? If we could only know, maybe it would be easier to "get on board" and "get on with life". As it stands, a few of us are probably a little nervous that it is all arbitrary and that saying "loved differently" is just a fancy way of saying "loved less". So, what motivates His choice? At the end of the day, we have to be honest, we do not know. "'For who has known the mind of the Lord, or who has been his counselor?'" (Rom 11:34). We believe, though, that His choice for this (and not that) is the issue of His infinite wisdom and His infinite love. "O the depth of the riches and wisdom and knowledge of God! How unsearchable are his judgments and how inscrutable his ways!" (Rom 11:33). If we can really trust that, we can be happy as a pinky toe or a patellar tendon.

Recall that God is at the center of the world, not us. He does what seems good to Him. He is the Creator; we are the creatures. We have to learn to be okay with that. "Am I not allowed to do what I choose with what belongs to me? Or do you begrudge my generosity?" (Mt 20:15). The goal of your life is that God would be loved, known, and glorified—by you, and through you. In light of this, the excellences of others are simply fuel for your fire: they are opportunities to praise God for a job well done, to rejoice that he is the kind of God who would make the Blessed Virgin Mary. "As for the saints in the land, they are the noble, in whom is all my delight" (Ps 16:3).

There is a place for a certain kind of "comparison", of course. We can look to others to be informed and inspired. When we read about the saints of the tradition, it can stir up a holy desire. We can say: "His witness really speaks to me. I cannot shake it. I cannot dismiss it. Perhaps, I ought to follow it." But we should never find ourselves dispirited or discouraged by the excellence of our brothers and sisters.

In other cases, we can simply say: "Wow. That is awesome. Clearly, the Lord has not willed those graces for me. But, he has willed them for her. And, because she and I are members of one body, I have them, too. May God be praised."

This approach helps us to appreciate how our brothers and sisters play a role in our salvation. As we mentioned just briefly, the glory of each Christian contributes to the glory of all the others. Each baptized person in the mystical body can enrich your life. In beholding the other, you behold, not a competitor for the love of God, but one who increases your capacity for love, your share of love. There is no shortage of grace to go around. It is not a scarce good. There is no risk that any one of us will use it all up, because its Source is infinite. Pseudo-Macarius writes:

> The brethren, therefore, regardless of what work they are doing, ought to conduct themselves toward each other in love and cheerfulness. And the one who works should say of him who is praying: "I also possess the treasure which my brother possesses since it is common." And let him who prays say of him who reads: "What he gains from reading redounds also to my advantage." And he who works let him thus say: "The work which I am doing is for the common good." For as the members of the body, being many, are one body (1 Cor 12:12) and help each other while each still performs its own function—as the eye sees for the whole body and the hand labors for all the members and the foot walks, sustaining all the members, and another member suffers with all the others—so also the brethren should be among themselves.[4]

This is what is meant by "love and cheerfulness". The gifts given to one are intended for all. "You received without

[4] Pseudo-Macarius, Homily 3.2, in *The Fifty Spiritual Homilies and the Great Letter*, trans. George A. Maloney, S.J. (New York: Paulist Press, 1992).

pay, give without pay" (Mt 10:8). When each conducts himself with generosity, the whole communion of saints is enriched. When I resent another's gifts, I reject my own—and thus I profit from neither. In the reign of envy, everyone loses.

It is not enough, however, merely to resign ourselves to our place and to quench the flames of envy. In order to find our fit and embrace our identity, we must learn how to *love* our place in the body—with all of its joys and difficulties. We will never be at peace if we strive for gifts not our own, if we go after things too great for us. "O LORD, my heart is not lifted up, my eyes are not raised too high; I do not occupy myself with things too great and too marvelous for me" (Ps 131:1). There is no sense lusting after graces that never were and never will be ours. A genuine openness to the gifts the Lord is actually giving allows us to assume our place within His body, playing our part within His plan.

With this in mind, you can learn to glory in your littleness. The graces that you receive, though they may seem modest by comparison to the graces that others receive, are those that God *actually* wills for you, those that God has "dreamt up" with you in mind. As such, they are ideal for you. It follows that God is most pleased, most glorified when you glory in these graces.

## Eucharistic Body, Mystical Body

Hopefully, we now have a clearer view of the goal, of the beautiful design God has for His Church. But how do we get there from where we are now? The answer should come as no surprise at this point: we get there through a life of Eucharistic worship.

When we receive the Eucharist, sacramentally and spiritually, we become what we receive—the body of Christ.

As we saw in chapter 4, it is a kind of "reverse digestion", as silly as that sounds. In our Eucharistic eating, Christ is the higher life form: He does not enter into us so much as we enter into Him, thus becoming one in His body. "The cup of blessing which we bless, is it not a participation in the blood of Christ? The bread which we break, is it not a participation in the body of Christ?" (1 Cor 10:16). We are made *one* in this body: "Because there is one bread, we who are many are one body, for we all partake of the one bread" (1 Cor 10:17).

With each Holy Communion, Saint Augustine preaches, we become who we are:

> So if it's you that are the body of Christ and its members, it's the mystery meaning you that has been placed on the Lord's table; what you receive is the mystery that means you. It is to what you are that you reply *Amen*, and by so replying you express your assent. What you hear, you see, is *The body of Christ*, and you answer, *Amen*. So be a member of the body of Christ, in order to make that *Amen* true.[5]

With each "Amen" pronounced in the sacred liturgy, we profess our faith in His Eucharistic body *and* His mystical body. The liturgy brings us before Christ present on the altar; in doing so, it brings us into His body the Church. The mysteries are inseparable. If we believe that "Truth himself speaks truly" of His Eucharistic body, then adoration should follow suit. If we believe that "Truth himself speaks truly" of His mystical body, then surrender ought to follow suit. If we are to become His mystical body, we must be incorporated into His higher life form; we must give way before His higher communion.

[5] Augustine of Hippo, Sermon 272, in *Sermons* III/7, trans. Edmund Hill, O.P. (New Rochelle, N.Y.: New City Press, 1993).

The Eucharistic elements tell the story of our transformation. As Saint Augustine writes:

> Remember that bread is not made from one grain, but from many.... He [Saint Paul] has already shown clearly enough what we should understand about the cup, even if it wasn't said. After all, just as many grains are mixed into one loaf in order to produce the visible appearance of bread, as though what holy scripture says about the faithful were happening: *They had one soul and one heart in God* (Acts 4:32); so too with the wine. Brothers and sisters, just remind yourselves what wine is made from; many grapes hang in the bunch, but the juice of the grapes is poured together in one vessel. That too is how the Lord Christ signified us, how he wished us to belong to him, how he consecrated the sacrament of our peace and unity on his table.[6]

If we are to form a single loaf (and cease to be a single grain), we can expect to be "ground", "leavened", and "baked". If we are to form a single chalice (and cease to be a single grape), we can expect to be "gathered", "crushed", and "fermented". The Lord welcomes your "active participation" in this transformation. So, too, He prompts your daily surrender as you assume your place within His mystical body. While this response may prove difficult at times, it ultimately leads to a discovery of your graces, your vocation, your identity, as one uniquely beloved and wholly belonging.

## Made Pure Bread

To conclude, I want to share a story from the early Church that sums up what we have been saying. In the second

[6] Ibid.

century, the bishop Saint Ignatius of Antioch was condemned to death for his Christian faith. Rather than have Saint Ignatius executed in his native Syria, ten soldiers escorted him across the empire to Rome, where he was eventually devoured by lions in the Colosseum.

As Saint Ignatius approached his appointment with death, he wrote several letters to encourage his fellow Christians. In one of those letters, he writes, "[P]ray leave me to be a meal for the beasts, for it is they who can provide my way to God. I am His wheat, ground fine by the lions' teeth to be made purest bread for Christ.... So intercede with Him for me, that by their instrumentality I may be made a sacrifice to God."[7] Saint Ignatius knew that the best way for him to become a true Christian was the way set before him. If he was to be a saint, he had to embrace his lot and abandon himself wholly to God. The circumstances helped him formulate his vocation with clarity and conviction. And in this desire, he was nourished by the Eucharist: "There is no pleasure for me in any meats that perish, or in the delights of this life; I am fain for the bread of God, even the flesh of Jesus Christ, who is the seed of David; and for my drink I crave that Blood of His which is love imperishable."[8] Note the familiar themes: union, sacrifice, love. Saint Ignatius wanted to become a true man, a true Christian. He wanted to live in union with Christ and His Church. In the death that lay before him, he found the perfect way to realize the transformation he so desired. And, in the Eucharist, he found the strength he needed to see it through, the infallible strength of love. To union through sacrifice in love.

[7] Ignatius of Antioch, "Epistle to the Romans", in *Early Christian Writings: The Apostolic Fathers*, trans. Maxwell Staniforth (New York: Penguin Books, 1987), 86.

[8] Ibid., 87.

So, though we may not follow the same road as Saint Ignatius, a similar transformation must take place in each of our lives. Like wheat ground to flour, whether by fierce persecution or the ordinary difficulties of Christian life, we must undergo a change. Only then can we hope to be made pure bread, only then can we hope to be offered. This is what we mean by surrender. As we let go of everything not of God—our false individualities, our envies and jealousies—we become who God intends. In this abandonment, we find our place in the mystical body—in union with Christ and in His Church. Thus it is that, already here on earth, we begin the heavenly life that lies beyond. In celebrating the sacred liturgy, we join the ranks of angels and saints gathered at the wedding feast of the lamb in heaven. We share in the cosmic liturgy of all creation, and we are transformed, little by little, into the one worshipping Christ.

# Chapter 8

# Keep Showing Up

Recently, I had a conversation with a woman who wanted a better approach to the faith. She felt that her spiritual life was lacking something. She was praying, making good use of the sacraments, and going on retreats, but it was not clicking somehow. She ought to have been making rapid progress, but she was not. A terrible ache resulted, a great longing for deeper intimacy with God that she was not able to realize.

The fact is, this woman had been living a good life. She had come a long way from where she started and already shown some real growth. What made her think that the current plateau was such a problem? Perhaps this, too, was a gift from God—something to clarify her faith, enrich her hope, intensify her love? If it was a gift, would it not be best to receive it?

Perhaps you have had similar thoughts about your own life, fighting the anxiety that you are missing out and falling short. Maybe you have read stacks of books about the spiritual life, hoping to find the one that finally cracks the code. You have grown tired of the same old exhortations to renewed fidelity and constancy. After all, in an age of conveniences, there must be something more, something better!

But, what if the Lord is just healing and growing us *in the way best known to Him*? Maybe the Lord is breaking us of a false sense of sanctity. Maybe He is teaching us not to confuse emotional highs with holiness. Maybe He is fostering in us a more radical dependence. God alone knows, and He knows best.

In the sacramental life of the Church, each of us has superabundant resources to spiritual growth. Even if we do not make perfect use of these resources at present, we can try to make better use of them with each passing day and leave the rest to God. Our prayer time may feel distracted or fatigued; it may be artificial or superficial—but this, too, can be saving if we accept everything from Him in a spirit of sacrifice, love, and self-abandonment.

## The Lord Gives the Growth

Paradoxically, obsession with spiritual growth can become an obstacle to real maturity, as we end up relying overly much on ourselves. The goal of the spiritual life is not an "A+" but union with God; and since He is infinite and we are finite, that union can only be brought about from above. At the end of the day, God will make us as holy as He makes us. He has concrete plans for us, and He will realize them in His time. Our job is to cooperate, to keep showing up, always remembering our spiritual poverty. As Saint Thérèse writes, "In the evening of this life, I shall appear before You with empty hands."[1] Our spiritual growth is His gift to give, His grace to bestow.

It can be comforting to think that we are in control. We like to think that spiritual growth is an item on *our*

[1] Thérèse of Lisieux, *Story of a Soul: The Autobiography of St. Thérèse of Lisieux*, trans. John Clarke, O.C.D., 3rd ed. (Washington, D.C.: ICS Publications, 1996), 277.

checklist. But the truth is far more comforting still: It is God who sees to your spiritual growth. As Saint Paul writes, "[God] desires all men to be saved and to come to the knowledge of the truth" (1 Tim 2:4). God desires your destiny more than you do. His will, which brought all things into being, is far more powerful than any desire you can muster.

If our hearts are to be made fit for perfect union, there is bound to be a process. The sadness, the loneliness, the anxiety—the various difficulties that we experience—are all part of our transformation. As we pass through present darkness, we have to trust that Christ is drawing us to the light and training our eyes along the way. He is preparing us for His fullness precisely *through* our present dissatisfaction. Our spiritual growth advances by clarifications and realizations all arranged to draw us deeper into the designs of His salvation and to give us a fuller share in it. If something new comes about, it is the Lord's doing. It is for us to be faithful and constant. "For thus said the Lord GOD, the Holy One of Israel, 'In returning and rest you shall be saved; in quietness and in trust shall be your strength'" (Is 30:15). The frantic search for a something lacking only distracts from the infinitely more beautiful pursuit of what God gives; namely, *His* growth in *His* time.

## Eucharistic Faith, Eucharistic Life

This transformation unfolds according to a sacramental pedagogy. Along the way, Christ has us return day in and day out to the Most Holy Eucharist. It seems monotonous, but it is profoundly *human*. In almost every sphere of human life, the way to perfection is remarkably monotonous. Much of our life is a matter of repetition, rehearsal, and maintenance. Our spiritual life is no different. God asks us to return to the source, to renew our devotion, to repeat our worship.

In order to make this "return" fruitful, however, we first need a solid foundation of faith. To embrace what is good, we have to believe it to be true. If the doctrine of the True Presence is not luminously evident to you, do not let this discourage you. Faith is a habit, and there are real things you can do to strengthen it.

For some of us, this will mean studying the mystery. Even if the intellectual side of the faith is not your strong suit, there is always something to be gained from inquiring further. Read a homily by one of the Church Fathers. Pick up a book on the theology of the Eucharist. The goal is not 100 percent comprehension but 100 percent immersion. Digging further into the mystery will also give you the confidence to provide reasons for your faith when you are called upon to do so; witnessing in this way will often, in turn, bolster your own belief.

Additionally, our bodies can be a tremendous asset in strengthening faith. Make the sign of the cross when you pass a Church; genuflect when you enter a space in which the Blessed Sacrament is reserved; bow when you pass before the tabernacle; in short, act like what you profess is true!

Perhaps most importantly, we need to *ask* for more faith. Throughout the day, make small acts of faith to reinforce and affirm your belief. Do not be embarrassed to pray aloud, even if under your breath. "Lord, I believe in you, present in the most Holy Sacrament of the altar." "Lord, I know that you are present in the Eucharist. Conform my life to this truth."

You might not *feel* like you know—but by the gift of faith at work in you, you *do* know. Throughout our lives, we have to return to the existential bedrock of divine testimony. As Saint Thomas writes, "I believe whatsoever the

Son of God has said | [for, there is] nothing truer than this word of Truth."[2] Our life ought to be governed by the urgency of this revelation. Faith is a choice. If we want to grow in Eucharistic devotion, we have to return again and again to belief and profession. On the foundation of a Eucharistic faith, you can start to build a Eucharistic life.

In the remaining pages, we will look at some practical ways to do this. As a preliminary note, however, remember what we said above: in all of this, God gives the growth. Yes, there is a necessary "purgation" whenever we seek deeper conversion—you have to address the obstacles that keep Christ from inhabiting your soul. That might mean saying "No" to certain invitations. It might mean turning off your devices. It might mean experiencing solitude, loneliness, even emptiness as you come into His holy presence. You will likely leave certain things, habits, and people behind. But living a Eucharistic life is not about all of the things you do to keep yourself in line and attain perfection. It is about having more of God and the things of God in your life. The soil of our soul is like a flower bed, and the weeds of sin will always pop up here and there. In addition to rooting up sin, we should be crowding it out, filling the soil of our soul with good seeds and bulbs. Then, we can leave behind sin and vice as we are occupied with the life of grace. If you fill your heart with all the fullness of God, there will be no room left for all that is not of Him.

## Regular Mass Attendance

At this stage of your conversion, you are probably already attending Mass a good bit. The Church asks us to attend

[2] Thomas Aquinas, *Adoro te devote*: "Credo quidquid dixit Dei Filius: nil hoc verbo Veritatis verius." (Translation mine.)

Mass on Sundays and on certain holy days. (Make sure you know what these are in your region!) In setting forth this precept, the Church speaks of our *obligation*. Many of us do not love the language of obligation. It can sound coercive. But worship is a *necessary* part of Christian life. If we want to safeguard our relationship with God, we have to go to Mass on Sundays and holy days. The Church's law works like a fence, showing the boundaries within which a genuine relationship can be found and maintained. It gives us certainty and confidence that we can abide in God.

Of course, Eucharistic worship goes beyond obligation. If we do only the obligatory things because they are obligatory, we miss the point. We are not just employees, and the Lord is not just our boss. "No longer do I call you servants, for the servant does not know what his master is doing; but I have called you friends, for all that I have heard from my Father I have made known to you" (Jn 15:15). We want to see our Eucharistic lives as an opportunity for intimacy, as a genuine invitation to greater spontaneity in relationship. Will there always be obligation in the background? Sure. But can there be a real adventure in the foreground? Yes! More frequent attendance at Mass and more frequent reception of Holy Communion are part of this adventure.

Many of you may attend daily Mass. If you do not, why not? That is not a subtle guilt trip. Many people are hesitant about daily Mass. Maybe you have just never thought of going. Maybe it is inconvenient or impossible given where you live, your various commitments, or your present circumstances. There are any number of reasons why people do not go. You do not have to feel guilty about that. The Church does not require you to go to daily Mass. Rather, the Lord invites you.

This is not an all-or-nothing proposal. Going to a few daily Masses does not mean you need to schedule it every day for the rest of your life. You can start small: go *sometimes* and see where it leads. You might choose a particular day of the week, commit to a special liturgical season, or make a "standing date" to attend with a friend. At my parish growing up, the 7:00 A.M. Mass was moved to 6:45 A.M. during Lent so that more commuters could attend. I used to go with my mom during high school, and she would treat me to bagels afterward. (Look, if an incentive like bagels gets you to Mass, no shame. Do what needs to be done.) I started attending daily Mass consistently at the invitation of my sister during college. The morning Mass at our university was the one time that our schedules always overlapped.

As you get into the habit, you may want to attend more frequently. Or you may not. The point is not to trick yourself into becoming a daily communicant. The point is to show up for the Holy Mass and see what God does with it. It is a tangible way of saying "Here I am, Lord." Daily Mass is not an obligation. It is an opportunity. You are genuinely free. Make use of your freedom, and leave it at that.

## Choosing a Church

The summer that I began to get excited about the priesthood, I was living in Portland, Maine. The local parish did not always have daily Mass, so I drove with my cousins to various churches in the area to fill out the week. The Jesuits on the north side of town had a convenient Mass with adoration afterward, so we went there often. I was impressed by how the priest handled the Eucharistic elements with tenderness, especially when purifying the vessels. We also went to a local Franciscan monastery for an evening Mass and Marian consecration once a week. There, I was moved by how the priests celebrated and preached with evident love for Our Lady. Then, the cathedral had the traditional Latin Mass on Sundays. There, I was gripped by the stark sacrificial logic of the liturgy. Each of these encounters helped me to discern my vocation as they cultivated in me a richer Eucharistic piety.

My point in telling this story is that your experience of the Mass hinges, in part, upon the parish you attend. Depending on the area in which you live and your access to transportation, you may have more or less choice in the matter, but it helps to ask yourself these questions about your local churches: Where is the Mass celebrated with reverence? Where does the preaching help me enter into the sacred mysteries? Where is there a community focused on Eucharistic worship and encouraging the same in visitors? Where is the liturgy most sublime—in the architecture, in the music, in the vestments and vessels? The point is not to become a critic or an aesthete. The point is to put ourselves and our families in contact with the beauty of the liturgy so that it can do its work effectively. (Especially for parents, it is crucial that you expose your children to Eucharistic devotion.)

Admittedly, we will always be dealing with obstacles. We ourselves bring plenty of obstacles wherever we go—our own sin and vice, our own fatigue and distraction. True devotion is an interior reality. Nevertheless, we are embodied beings, and we have a much better chance of worshipping well when we attend a Mass that is celebrated well. The reverence of the Mass, the preaching of the ministers, the community life of the parish, and the beauty of the space are all important factors in maturing in your Eucharistic identity.

## Confessing Your Sins

Once you have resolved to attend Mass, how do you prepare for Holy Communion? A good first step is to deal with big sins: "So if you are offering your gift at the altar, and there remember that your brother has something against you, leave your gift there before the altar and go; first be reconciled to your brother, and then come and offer your gift" (Mt 5:23–24). If you have committed a mortal sin since your last Confession, head to the sacrament of Penance as soon as you are able. Meanwhile, attend Mass but do not receive Holy Communion. For many of you, that may be uncomfortable. Perhaps someone has told you that you can just make a good act of contrition, present yourself for Communion, and go to Confession at the next opportunity. This has never been the Church's official teaching, and I would advise you against this practice. While we do not always know how badly we have sinned, especially if our knowledge or consent is compromised (by addiction, for instance), we should assume that a sin involving grave matter is mortal and that we are not in a state to receive.

It takes real integrity to abstain from Holy Communion when in an unworthy state. The Lord gives us this grace when we ask for it, and He uses these opportunities to make us even more steadfast in our worship. This honesty helps mature us in our conversion and address the abiding causes of sin and vice in our lives; it helps us to "feel" more concretely the separation from God that we ourselves have introduced through our transgressions. For those struggling with habitual mortal sin, a regular confessor can help you determine a reasonable frequency for the sacrament of Confession to ensure regular reception of Holy Communion without falling into scrupulosity.

Our use of the sacrament of Penance is not limited to times when it is strictly necessary, such as when we are conscious of mortal sin. You can *always* benefit from sacramental absolution. When you are not aware of any mortal sins, you can still make what is called a "devotional

Confession" in which you recount more recent venial sins or less recent mortal sins (from past Confessions). The idea is to get more fine-grained with your acknowledgment of present sins and to renew your sorrow for and hatred of past sins. The sacrament of Penance is not just a reset button, squaring us with God for the moment. It is also a source of grace and especially the grace of penitence.

This spirit of penitence helps us to approach the altar intentionally and attentively. It makes us aware of our unworthiness, alerting us to the ways we have set up obstacles to God's work in our lives. It stirs up grace and virtue in our lives, sending us back to Eucharistic worship with a renewed sense of urgency and of our need for God's abundant mercy. When we receive Holy Communion with penitence, it gives us a greater appreciation for the gift of divine life and for Christ's generosity in instituting this sacrament.

To stir up this Eucharistic penitence, establish a regular habit of sacramental Confession. The Church requires us to go at least once a year when conscious of mortal sin. Every saint I know of has gone far more often. If we want to be saints, why not follow in their footsteps? Saint Carlo Acutis, who lived a radiantly Eucharistic life, says we should go once a week. The Second Vatican Council asks consecrated religious to go once every two weeks. To start, I would recommend that you go at least once a month. In conversation with your pastor or your spiritual director, you might decide to go more or less frequently as befits your spiritual growth.

## Maintaining Peace

Okay, you are attending Mass regularly. You are confessing your sins faithfully. What is next? Let's focus on guarding your peace. It is hard to enter into the celebration of the Mass when we are distracted and dispersed. Maybe you have got a billion things going on today. Maybe you just received an inscrutable text message and cannot fathom what it means. Maybe you are in the middle of a tense interpersonal conflict and cannot think of anything else. The fact is that Christ extends the gift of His peace: "Peace I leave with you; my peace I give to you; not as the world gives do I give to you. Let not your hearts be troubled" (Jn 14:27). There will always be an excuse to refuse this gift, but we do so only to our own harm.

Cultivating recollection is not about playing defense against distraction or scrambling to maintain a prayerful spirit. The traditional wisdom is that you will always be on defense until you go on offense. We have to frame our Eucharistic lives with a border of peace. Saint Charles Borromeo writes this about the unrecollected priest: "As soon as he comes into church ... to celebrate Mass, a thousand thoughts fill his mind and distract him from God. But what was he doing in the sacristy before he came out for the office or for Mass? How did he prepare? What means did he use to collect his thoughts and to remain recollected?"[3] The same questions can be asked of the unrecollected parishioner. What were you thinking of in the parking lot, on the way to church, or at home upon rising?

If we are going to stand a chance of being recollected at Mass, it cannot be the only time that we are recollected. Recollection should characterize the whole of our day. That sounds like a tall order, especially with all of life's demands and the speed at which our world moves. But here

[3] Charles Borromeo, *Acta Ecclesiae Mediolanensis* (1599), in *The Liturgy of the Hours*, vol. 4, trans. ICEL, Office of Readings for the Memorial of Saint Charles Borromeo (New York: Catholic Book Publishing, 1975), 1544.

the Mass can stabilize us. Eucharistic worship is like a rally point from which God mounts His offensive, extending His dominion into further and further reaches of our soul. And with His dominion come recollection and peace.

Throughout the day, try to keep Mass in mind. Think forward to Mass and back to Mass. Saint John Paul II said, "Holy Mass is the absolute center of my life and of every day of my life."[4] We aim to live with a similar focus. How can you lessen the stress in the moments leading up to Mass? How can you leave space to reflect more on its gifts and graces? The conclusions that you draw may require real changes in your life—in how you interact with your phone and your computer, in how you consume news and entertainment, in how you structure your day, in how you eat, drink, smoke, and so on. The Lord wants to get into all of these details with you. You just need to pose the question to Him and wait on His answer.

For bolstering our peace and entering into Eucharistic worship, however, there is no better support than a daily habit of prayer. Saint Paul writes: "The Lord is at hand. Have no anxiety about anything, but in everything by prayer and supplication with thanksgiving let your requests be made known to God. And the peace of God, which passes all understanding, will keep your hearts and your minds in Christ Jesus" (Phil 4:5–7). Note the logic of Paul's encouragement: it is the presence of God that dispels our anxieties, and it is in prayer that we enter into this saving presence. Prayer is the heartbeat of our spiritual circulation, the sustenance of our spiritual energy. Prayer, as the saints teach, is a simple exchange between the soul and God. In this exchange, we come to discover who God is and who we are. Prayer also gives us insight into

[4] *L'Osservatore Romano*, English edition, November 15, 1995, p. 7.

the wisdom and love animating God's plan, helping us to abandon ourselves more wholly to Him.

Eucharistic worship builds on the foundation of habitual prayer. If we want to attend Mass devoutly and receive Holy Communion fruitfully, it starts with a *life* of prayer. Mass is the highest expression of prayer, to be preferred to all other prayers. As the Fathers of the Second Vatican Council clarify: "Popular devotions of the Christian people are to be highly commended.... But these devotions should be so drawn up that they harmonize with the liturgical seasons, accord with the sacred liturgy, are in some fashion derived from it, and lead the people to it, since, in fact, the liturgy by its very nature far surpasses any of them."[5] Nevertheless, we cannot treat the Mass as if it were magically all-sufficient. Mass will not necessarily furnish you with an interior life if you only ever approach in a spirit of commotion. Attending Mass and receiving Holy Communion should represent the sacramental consummation of a contemplative life, not the exclusive exercise of one's spiritual life.

As you strive to guard your peace, do not worry too much about the inevitable setbacks. We all fail, and we should not be surprised when it happens. The evil one wants us to rely wholly on ourselves so that we are discouraged when trials arise. But God can use all things for His glory and our salvation. Once we recognize our unconversion, we can simply call on the mercy of God, take the sacramental steps, and renew our intention.

Insofar as you are able, try to arrive early to Mass. There are some religious communities who have a practice of arriving early to the chapel just so they can wait outside the door together for a few minutes. They know that it takes a

[5] Second Vatican Council, *Sacrosanctum Concilium* (December 4, 1963), §13.

few minutes to recollect themselves, and so they built that time into their schedule. After they have taken some deep breaths and asked God to set aside their various worries, they enter the chapel together for liturgical prayers.

## Eating the Word

One of the best things you can do to cultivate this interior stillness is to arrive a few minutes early for Mass. I get it: many of us are battling a never-ending list of tasks, the allure of constant productivity. I challenge you to break out of task-management mode for the minutes leading up to Mass. If our standard for the whole of the day is efficiency, we will always be tempted to understand our spiritual lives in terms of efficiency. Of its very nature, the liturgy pushes back against this error. The point is not efficiency, but presence. God is present to us that we might be present to Him.

Now, once you have arrived early at Mass, you can take that time for some further preparation. I recommend that you read the readings of the day and pray with them a bit. The daily readings narrate God's plans for the salvation of the world *today*. They are addressed to you, personally, and you have to get quiet enough to listen. There may be some readings that resonate more. There might be some readings that resonate less. All the Church asks of us is to listen and see what comes of listening.

Maybe your kids are acting up during the first reading. Maybe you miss the psalm response a few times before remembering it. Maybe the Gospel is just so familiar that you tune out. Still, the Church asks us to pay attention, because these words are an essential part of the spiritual meal that is the Mass. "Man shall not live by bread alone, but by every word that proceeds from the mouth of God"

(Mt 4:4). So, while it may be easy to zone out, we have to keep coming back with a desire to draw life from the Scriptures. Reading the readings ahead of time can help us in this. To that end, consider investing in a hand missal or a subscription to a worship aid like *Magnificat*.

Reviewing the daily readings can also help you formulate an intention for the Mass. There are bound to be certain things for which or certain people for whom you are praying irrespective of the daily readings. But, if you are attentive to the Word, you might find that the Scriptures prompt you to ask for peculiar graces or virtues or to pray for a particular family member or friend. The Word continues to speak into our concrete circumstances; it is "living and active" (Heb 4:12). By giving some time and space to the sacred page, we enter more heartily into God's plans for us.

A last word on hand missals and worship aids. My recommendation is to avoid reading along during the Mass itself. When I proclaim the Gospel, it feels strange to behold a congregation of people all looking down and reading along. It feels disconnected from the liturgical action. The Church teaches that the proclamation of the Word is an ongoing act of revelation. God addresses His people in the liturgical assembly. When we look away from the liturgical action, it can alter the way we register this encounter. It is a little like watching a movie with subtitles. Some of us have come to rely on captions. Maybe our hearing is not what it used to be; maybe the actors mumble or fail to project; maybe we are working on mastering a second language. But whatever the reason, I suspect most of us would acknowledge it is not an ideal state of affairs. Movies and shows are not meant to be watched with subtitles. We are meant to look at the actors, to see their faces and gestures. So, too, in the sacred liturgy. God intends us to follow the liturgical action with utmost attention; it is in this action that He comes to meet us. Missals and worship aids should facilitate that encounter, insofar as possible. They should not replace it.

## The Mass Is Its Own Preparation

As we make our preparations for Mass, we need to keep in mind a simple but easily forgotten truth: the Mass itself is the best preparation for reception of Holy Communion. The liturgy takes us by the hand and leads us into the fullness of Eucharistic worship. Every detail is carefully designed to ready your heart to be united to Christ in the Eucharist. At the beginning of each Mass, in the "penitential rite", we repent before the most-high God as we pray for healing and mercy. Then, we listen attentively to the Sacred Scriptures, as we ask for illumination and conversion through the divine Word. As the priest prepares the altar, we join our sacrifice to his and commend our offering to God. We then progress through the prayers of the Mass and arrive at the Consecration. The prayers of the Mass are not "fillers" around the main event. They are intended to make us ready for the Lord's coming, so we should listen. The Mass *is* our preparation. All of the other efforts we have described should be directed to the Mass, oriented to help us intend and attend with greater abandon.

Each Mass, moreover, is the best preparation for the next one. Each time we receive Holy Communion, we are preparing to receive Holy Communion again. Conscious of this fact, we should make an effort to thank God for what we have received so that we are better disposed to receive again. You have probably heard people talk about "making a thanksgiving". At the conclusion of Mass, you can just remain in your pew for a few minutes and thank God. This might be hard at first if folks start chatting in the body of the church at the end of Mass, but you might find that, in time, others are prompted by your example. I went to Franciscan University of Steubenville, and making a thanksgiving was very much part of the liturgical culture. Many of those in attendance would linger to thank God even if that meant they were farther back in line at the dining hall. I started making a thanksgiving in deference to pious peer pressure. Gradually, it became a matter of sincere devotion. If you do not know exactly what to say, you might simply memorize one of the prayers of thanksgiving written by the various saints in the tradition. (You will be surprised to learn that I memorized the one written by Saint Thomas Aquinas.)

You may have heard that in the Church's history, daily reception of Holy Communion was not always encouraged among lay Catholics. The fear was that daily reception could easily become routine reception for which one did not prepare or give thanks. By arriving a little early and staying a little late, and by faithfully following the words and actions of the liturgy, we can safeguard a sense of Eucharistic amazement so that the fear of empty routines is adequately addressed.

## Adoring the Blessed Sacrament

Even when we arrive early and stay late, however, the Mass does not always leave us lots of time to unpack this Eucharistic encounter. Pope Benedict XVI writes, "Communion only reaches its true depths when it is supported and surrounded by adoration."[6] In adoration, we have all the time in the world to prolong our Eucharistic worship.

[6]Joseph Ratzinger, *The Spirit of the Liturgy: Commemorative Edition* (San Francisco: Ignatius Press, 2018), 104.

In adoration, we enter into God's holy presence with a simple desire to pass the time together.

Now, one might say, "Is God not already everywhere? Why should I pray in the church when I can just pray in my car or in my bedroom?" Certainly, God is present everywhere, but He is *more* present in the Most Holy Eucharist. The Eucharist extends the Incarnation; it extends Christ's bodily presence. Think about it this way: During His earthly life, Christ—as God—was equally present to all places on the surface of the earth. Nevertheless, He was *more* present to His mother and His disciples in His sacred humanity. We sense, intuitively, that there was something especially intimate about gathering with Him on the shore of the Sea of Galilee or in the Upper Room. In drawing near to the Blessed Sacrament, we share in that same intimacy. We draw near to Christ in the place where He is most present on earth.

Many of us sense this without even realizing it. In a church where the Blessed Sacrament is reserved, we are careful to avoid talking; we cross the sanctuary with respect, even on tip-toe; we remove hats and leave behind mundane conversation. Now, think of the strange experience of Good Friday. When the Blessed Sacrament is removed from the church, it is as if the air has gone out of the room. We feel the difference immediately and acutely. The church loses its warmth, its welcome. What formerly felt like a home now feels like a tomb. Christ's presence, while intangible, is somehow palpable.

In the months leading up to her conversion, Saint Elizabeth Ann Seton started to experience a longing for the Lord's Eucharistic presence. Even while still attending Protestant services, she began reorienting her worship. "I got into a side pew which turned my face toward the Catholic church in the next street, and twenty times found myself speaking to the Blessed Sacrament there instead of looking at the naked altar before me...."[7] It is hard to explain, but there is something to His presence that draws our gaze.

We can encounter Jesus in the tabernacle in any open church. The simplicity of a Eucharistic visit (even a short one) and the devotion that informs it can make all the difference. You may have noticed that I have made no mention of a monstrance yet. That is on purpose. We can adore the Blessed Sacrament regardless of whether or not it is exposed. Many prefer adoration of the exposed Blessed Sacrament (and with good cause), but we should not lose sight of the importance of adoration of the non-exposed Blessed Sacrament. The simple closeness of His Eucharistic body is good. The Lord invites us to draw near to the sacrament of His fiery charity that we might partake of its illumination and warmth. Truth be told, it is not terribly clear what goes on in our exchange with Jesus. You might kneel; you might sit. You might say a little; you might say a lot. You might remain attentive; you might drift or snooze. One thing is sure though: life is better when spent close to Him.

There was a time in my life during which I had great difficulty sleeping. I tried reading boring books or praying the Rosary in bed with the hope that I would fall asleep eventually. More often than not, though, I would see through my own ruses and end up more agitated (and wired) than before. Early on, I happened upon a solution: Go to the Blessed Sacrament. The chapel was the one place in which I could just give up—give up trying

[7] Elizabeth Ann Seton, "Letter to Amabilia Filicchi on 25 September 1804," in Madame de Barberey, *Elizabeth Seton*, trans. Joseph B. Code (New York: Macmillan, 1927), 119.

to sleep, give up trying to trick myself, give up stressing about present anxiety or future fatigue. I could just give up in the Lord's presence. And, as it turned out, I would often fall asleep.

With my newfound strategy, I then tried to *use* the chapel as a sedative, but once I started to manipulate the conditions, it did not work in the same way. The Lord's Eucharistic presence was not to be used, as if sleep were a higher good than adoration. My sleeplessness was an invitation to adoration. If sleep followed, well, then God be praised. If sleep did not follow, well, then God be praised.

## Held in His Gaze

I have spent a lot of time stressing and anguishing in the presence of the Blessed Sacrament. I think part of what I love so much about bringing my little difficulties to the Eucharistic Lord is that, in Him, I discover God's response to my isolation. "I will not leave you desolate; I will come to you" (Jn 14:18). In the various ordeals of human life, perhaps the most acute suffering is the experience of isolation. We can often endure incredible pain and loss when surrounded by loved ones; not so when we feel alone. In the thick of life's trials, we lean on friends who help smooth out the rough patches and sweeten the bitterness. As Chesterton once wrote, "There are no words to express the abyss between isolation and having one ally."[8] Jesus desires to be our one ally, and His presence in the Eucharist is our proof. As Saint Margaret Mary Alacoque encourages each of us: "We must never be discouraged

[8] G.K. Chesterton, *The Man Who Was Thursday: A Nightmare* (Mattituck, N.Y.: Amereon House, 1908), 89.

or give way to anxiety ... but ever have recourse to the adorable Heart of Jesus."[9]

This does not mean that we "use" Jesus to cure ourselves. I do not rely upon my friends simply to troubleshoot my problems. Rather, I look to them because they are closer to me than my sorrows. In the midst of great trials, there is a kind of fear that whatever this affliction is, it is the most characteristic thing about me. It seems closer to me than I am to myself. A cry rises to my lips, "Wretched man that I am! Who will deliver me from this body of death?" (Rom 7:24). In that moment, to have someone who is truly present to us in our sorrow makes all the difference. Christ wants to be present to us in this way. As the author of *In Sinu Jesu* hears from the Lord: "I am He who understands every man's loneliness.... I want to share their loneliness so that they will not be alone with themselves, but alone with Me. There I shall speak to their hearts as I am speaking to you."[10]

In the midst of our sorrows, the Lord introduces Himself as our friend. In Eucharistic adoration, He draws closer to me than my stress, than my anxiety, than my sorrow, than my confusion and uncertainty about who I am or where my life is going. He draws closer to me than I do to myself. He gets beneath the weight and sin that cling so close, creating space between me and everything else that threatens to crowd out my true character. From the tabernacle and the monstrance, He gazes into my life, undeterred by distraction, engrossed with attention. In His gaze, I find my identity, my Eucharistic identity.

[9] Emily Jaminet, *Secrets of the Sacred Heart: Twelve Ways to Claim Jesus' Promises in Your Life* (Notre Dame, IN: Ave Maria Press, 2020), 108.

[10] A Benedictine Monk, *In Sinu Jesu: When Heart Speaks to Heart* (Brooklyn, N.Y.: Angelico Press, 2016), 14.

His attention in turn begets our own. Our response to Him is not so much the fruit of many efforts as it is the recognition of an offer that goes before us. Eucharistic worship is but the heart's captivation with Christ who attends to us. If He is so really and truly present to us, why not spend our lives trying to be wholly present to Him? "He looks at me, and I look at Him." There are no words to express the abyss between averting our eyes and holding His gaze. For, in His presence, there is no isolation that our divine Friend does not inhabit. If we are to lay claim to our true identity, we must seek to cultivate this Eucharistic gaze.

You are not made to search endlessly for a secret never to be found. The only secret of your life is Christ. In His gaze, there is neither missing out nor falling short. In His gaze, there is *nothing* lacking. In Him you have everything, and yourself besides. In the most Blessed Sacrament, He bares His heart before you. Will you risk baring yours in return?